Mad Doctors, Monsters and Mummies!

Lobby Card Posters from Hollywood Horrors!

A DENIS GIFFORD COLLECTION

BLOSSOM

ISBN 1 872532 59 4

Photography by Derek Smith and Jay Tauben

Design: Roger Lightfoot

Typeset in Great Britain by Uppercase

Printed and bound in Hong Kong

H. C. Blossom
6/7 Warren Mews
London W1P 5DJ

Contents

The selection of lobby cards is arranged in chronological order of the films' release dates.

What is a Lobby Card?

A Lobby Card is a thing of beauty and a joy for ever. Well – now then! Not many of my personal collection of lobby cards could be called things of beauty, but certainly there is joy for ever to be found in contemplating them. Whether they be photographic, artwork, or an odd mixture of both, a look at a lobby card will bring back to your mind the joys of the film it advertises – if you have seen the film, of course. Or, and more likely than not, it will make you damned glad you never wasted your time, not to mention your hard-earned one-and-ninepence on such obvious rubbish!

But if you are a true Movie Buff, the kind that once haunted your local Gaumont, Odeon and ABC in the days when there were three distinct and rival circuits of cinemas, or more so if you were the even truer kind of Movie Buff, the kind that queued at your nearest Essoldo, Tolmer or Golden Domes, then you won't wish you had seen the worst of the films represented here – you *will* have seen them! You will have sorted them out in the small print of your local *Sydenham, Forest Hill and Penge Gazette* (ah, even the titles of bygone newspapers had a ring to them seldom sounded nowadays!), and made dangerous voyages across town and country by bus and tram to where long-forgotten flea-pits and bug-hutches once lurked rather shamefacedly up side-streets.

Once esconced a bit tippily in an unstuffed fauteuil with your greasy bag of warmed-over salted peanuts from Woolworth's, or, if it was wartime, your little tubular packet of unrationed Jasco Mints, you escaped Attlee's austerity into Hollywood's heaven: three hours or more of Big Pictures (starring George Brent, Ida Lupino and the neckless Edward S. Brophy), Little Pictures (starring Regis Toomey, Veda Ann Borg and the crinkle-haired Frank Jenks), British Movietonews ('Leslie Mitchell reporting'), Pathé Pictorials ('This week's stars, the Two Leslies singing "Teas, Light Refreshments and Minerals"!'), and Signs of the Times ('Today we visit the Ovaltine Dairy Farm'). And, of course, those wonderful trailers ('Next Sunday for One Day Only'), which meant you simply had to come back again All Next Week or you would miss the World's Greatest Double Feature. (Wait a minute, didn't last week's say that about *this* week's films?)

Lobby Cards are, in a way, trailers; coloured cardboards luring you into the cashbox where you pays your money and takes your choice, of seat, if not of film. They were nearly always in colour, of course, often a strange, flat, blobbing sort of colour that always reminded me of our annual school photographs. Rather reminiscent of the early stencil-colour system applied to silent films by batteries of ladies with small brushes, samples of which occasionally survive and are shown by Film Archives. A few lobby cards were even coloured on the backs! This was for a type of display cabinet illuminated from behind, so that the colours showed through the cardboard. The point is that with all these coloured lobby cards, nobody to my knowledge ever complained to the manager that the films themselves turned out to be black-and-white . Perhaps we were so used to virtually all films being made in monochrome in those days, we took coloured stills for granted. The odd thing is that in later times, not so long ago in fact, I was asked to lend a Charlie Chaplin still to the *TV Times* to promote the showing of one of his features on Channel Four. It was rejected on the grounds that the advertisement I sent them was in colour, and the film was in black-and-white!

Horror films, to which this particular selection is devoted, were always made in monochrome, of course. There still persists the rumour that the 1931 *Frankenstein* was first shown tinted green, but that seems more like a lighting effect applied by the cinema manager. A couple of Warner Brothers' early efforts were in two-tone technicolor, and debate still rages among the fans as to whether *Dr Cyclops*, Paramount's 1939 saga of shrinking persons, should be classed as a horror or a science-fiction film. Perhaps the award for being first in colour horror should go to the minor *Scared to Death* (1947), a Bela Lugosi vehicle made by Golden Gate Productions and included here. It was not until the British studio of Hammer Film Productions got going on their series of classic remakes that technicolor entered the horror film repertoire and remained to stay. (British horror films are not to be found herein; they await their own collation later.)

Stereoscopy, call it Three-Dimensional, Natural Vision, or what you will, was an early Fifties craze which brought new life to the horror film, although not all the Hollywood 3-D horrors were shown that way in the UK. *House of Wax*, the Warner remake of *The Mystery of the Wax Museum*, was, and its lobby card is here. But although the card does its darndest to illustrate the third dimensional effect, it has in fact been doctored by the cinema that showed it; they showed it 'flat'. Another bit of doctoring is demonstrated here by the lobby card for Columbia's *The Werewolf*. A rather large strip obscures one eye of the afflicted hero with the

What is a Lobby Card?

words, 'Classified by Ontario Board of Film Censors as Adult Entertainment'. How different from the publicity attached to the card for a double feature, *The Vampire's Coffin* and *The Robot Versus the Aztec Mummy:* 'Recommended by the Young America Horror Club'. This was a non-existent outfit set up by the distributors, Young America Productions!

Other oddities among this necessarily short survey of an era that spanned thirty or more years include one of William Castle's curiosities. Castle was a plumpish, cigar-puffing semi-impresario who, after a fairly decent career turning out B-thrillers at Columbia, set himself up as a producer-director with a string of oddball low budgeters, each of which had a different gimmick. These gimmicks even reached Great Britain. I recall quite vividly a visit to the Essoldo, Penge, to see one in which a dangling white skeleton on a string came trundling out of the side curtain during the film, jiggled over a few rows of the audience, and jerked back again. I often wondered whether the ice-cream girl got an extra bob or two for lending a cranking hand, or if the manager had to do it himself to avoid a strike. I don't think William Castle travelled around with the print. That stunt was called "Filmed in Emergo!" The Castle curiosity depicted here is *The Tingler,* which is the one where a few seats in the auditorium were wired with vibrators, a word then unconnected with any form of female artificial stimulation, so nobody was shocked morally, only physically. The cunning Castle got round the obvious expense of wiring every seat in the cinema by putting up a poster saying that only those truly sensitive to attacks by a Tingler would be affected. Clever chap, Castle.

Roger Corman, of course, the man that brought Edgar Allan Poe-try suitably expanded into screen form, and gave Vincent Price virtually a new career as the world's number one horror star, figures largely here with films from both ends of the Corman scale: low-budget and low-low budget. Both provided a lot of fun and it seems sad that his many, many pictures in both the horror and sci-fi genres have seldom if ever been shown on British television. Perhaps the Young America Horror Club will rise up and attack our TV stations with Tinglers.

Denis Gifford

MISCHA AUER

in

The MONSTER WALKS

The Monster Walks

UK title The Monster Walked
1932 Action Pictures
Distributor Mayfair
Producer Cliff Broughton
Director Frank R. Strayer
Screenplay Robert Ellis
Camera Jules Cronjager
Editor Byron Robinson
Assistant Director Vernon Keayes
70 minutes

Rex Lease Ted Clayton
Vera Reynolds Ruth Earlton
Sheldon Lewis Robert Earlton
Mischa Auer Hanns Krug
Martha Mattox Mrs Krug
Sidney Bracy Herbert Wilkes
Sleep'n'Eat (Willie Best) Exodus

'Twas a dark and stormy night when pretty young heroine Ruth Earlton (Vera Reynolds), accompanied by handsome young hero Ted Clayton (Rex Lease), returns to her spooky old home to hear the reading of her dead dad's will. She inherits everything, money and crumbling property, save for a small slice which goes to faithful old housekeeper, Mrs Krug (Martha Mattox). In the event of Ruth's demise, everything will then go to her uncle. Fortunately he is an ageing paralytic confined to his wheelchair, but since he is played by Sheldon Lewis, all may not be well, as those with long cinematic memories might suspect. Uncle Robert is played by a man who played both kindly medico and evil other half in the 1920 version of *Dr Jekyll and Mr Hyde*. Hanns Krug, the housekeeper's son, is also Uncle Bob's son, which may account for his sinister mien. He is played by Mischa Auer, after this 1932 movie to be known as a fine Hollywood comedian. What with a fright-bound Negro servant called Exodus, played by an actor called Sleep'n'Eat, and a monster gorilla chained in a cage in the cellar, the film was so antiquated by the time it was released in the UK (held up for seven years by the censor), and so severely shortened by ten minutes, that the British distributors, Federated Films, recommened that its 'H' for Horrific certificate be publicised as 'H' for Hilarity.

THE MONSTER AND THE Girl

with

ELLEN DREW · ROBERT PAIGE · PAUL LUKAS
ROD CAMERON · PHILLIP TERRY · GEORGE ZUCCO
JOSEPH CALLEIA · ONSLOW STEVENS
A PARAMOUNT PICTURE

Directed by Stuart Heisler
Original Screen Play by Stuart Anthony

The Monster and the Girl

1940 Paramount Pictures
Producer Jack Moss
Director Stuart Heisler
Story from the silent screenplay
Go and Get It by Marion Fairfax
Screenplay Stuart Anthony
Camera Victor Milner
Art Directors Hans Dreier,
          Haldane Douglas
Editor Everett Douglas
Musical Director Sigmund Krumgold
65 minutes

Ellen Drew *Susan Webster*
Robert Paige *Larry Reed*
Paul Lukas *Bruhl*
Joseph Calleia *Deacon*
Onslow Stevens *J. Stanley McMasters*
George Zucco *Dr Parry*
Rod Cameron *Sam Daniels*
Philip Terry *Scott Webster*
Marc Lawrence *Sleeper*
Gerald Mohr *Munn*
Tom Dugan *Capt Alton*
Willard Robertson *Lt Strickland*
Minor Watson *Judge Pulver*
George Meader *Dr Knight*
Cliff Edwards *Leon Stokes*
Edward Van Sloane *Warden*
Abner Biberman *Gregory*
Skipper *the Dog*

From out of the swirling mists she comes to talk direct to the nervous audience. 'My name is Susan Webster,' she begins, and then tells us the strange, mysterious, unbelievable story of what happened to her brother's brain. A doctor put it into a gorilla's head! Not too surprising when we see that the doctor in question is none other than George Zucco, the deceptively urbane English gentleman with the balefully glistening eyeballs. Not too unbelievable, either, if you happened to be old enough to go to the pictures in 1920. A silent film called *Go and Get It* told a remarkably similar story, but there was nothing on the credits of this film to tell you that. These remakes were a common enough occurrence among the B-movies of the Forties, but somehow one expected more from Paramount, a studio that had been well to the fore in the first horror film boom of the Thirties. Indeed, their *Island of Lost Souls* (Charles Laughton and Bela Lugosi out of H.G. Wells) had been instantly banned by the British Board of Film Censors. Philip Terry, who played Ellen Drew's electrocuted but innocent brother, dies early in the film, but his brain lives on in the skull of Zucco's ape as he clambers around the rooftops wreaking vengeance on Paul Lukas and his gangsters. Only Skipper the dog watched and waited.

Bowery at Midnight

1942 Banner Productions
Distributor Monogram Pictures
Producers Sam Katzman, Jack Dietz
Associate Producer Barney A. Sarecky
Director Wallace Fox
Story Sam Robins
Screenplay Gerald Schnitzler
Camera Mack Stengler
Art Director David Milton
Editor Carl Pierson
Music Edward J. Kay
61 minutes

Bela Lugosi *Prof. Brenner/Wagner*
John Archer *Richard Dennison*
Wanda McKay *Judy Malvern*
Tom Neal *Frankie Mills*
Vince Barnett *Charlie*
John Berkes *Finger Dolan*
Ray Miller *Big Man*
J. Farrell MacDonald *Capt. Mitchell*
Lew Kelly *Doc Brooks*
Lucille Vance *Mrs Malvern*
Anna Hope *Mrs Brenner*
Wheeler Oakman

In 1939 Bela Lugosi, once a striking Count Dracula, came to England to play a double role in Edgar Wallace's *Dark Eyes of London*. He was both an insurance broker and a kindly, whiskery old dear who ran a home for the handicapped. In neither role was he up to any good. Three years later, back home in Hollywood, Lugosi turns up in *Bowery at Midnight*, cast as both Professor Brenner, a university authority on psychology, and Karl Wagner, who runs a mission for the underprivileged of the Bowery slums. In either role he is up to his worst. Now there's a coincidence, as comedian Harold Berens used to exclaim! Lugosi forces those ex-jailbreakers among his residents to return to their lives of crime, stealing gems for him. If they refuse, he hands their corpses over to Doc Brooks, the demented drug-addict who runs a sinister hospital underneath the floorboards. Brooks shows his dislike of Wagner by reviving the victims and keeping them prisoner in a pit. In a grand finale, Brooks refuses to kill the heroine and pushes Lugosi into the pit where he meets a howling death at the hands of the living dead.

PRESENTED BY WARNER BROS.

THE HIDDEN HAND

The Hidden Hand

1942 Warner Brothers
Producer William Jacobs
Director Ben Stoloff
Story from Invitation to Murder
by Bradley King
Screenplay Anthony Coldeway,
Raymond L. Schrock
Camera Henry Sharp
Art Director Stanley Fleischer
Editor Harold McLernon
68 minutes

Craig Stevens *Peter Thorne*
Elisabeth Fraser *Mary Winfield*
Julie Bishop *Rita*
Willie Best *Eustace*
Frank Wilcox *Lawrence*
Cecil Cunningham *Lorinda Channing*
Ruth Ford *Estelle*
Milton Parsons *John Channing*
Roland Drew *Walter Channing*
Tom Stevenson *Horace Channing*
Maria Hall *Eleanor Stevens*
Inez Geray *Hattie*
Kam Tong *Mallo*

Milton Parsons was that chap who, more than any other Hollywood small part player, cornered the medicinal market in morgue attendants throughout the Forties. His long, lugobrious features, rolling eyes and wobbly mouth in a cadaverous, balding head that looked as if it would roll off his neck at any moment, made him ideally suited for the role, guaranteeing a nervous laugh from any audience, which was all that any B-movie director could want. Although listed way down at number eight, his usual cast position, this little chiller is Parson's monument. He plays John Channing, weirdest of the Channing clan, for he is an incarcerated lunatic. Escaping early on in the epic, he poses as the Channing family butler, enabling him to lurk about the shadows in suitably sinister fashion, strangling whomsoever the scriptwriter fancies, while dowager Cecil Cunningham, playing his wealthy sister Lorinda, runs a simple test to discover which member of her large family should inherit her fortune. She puts herself into suspended animation and plays dead.

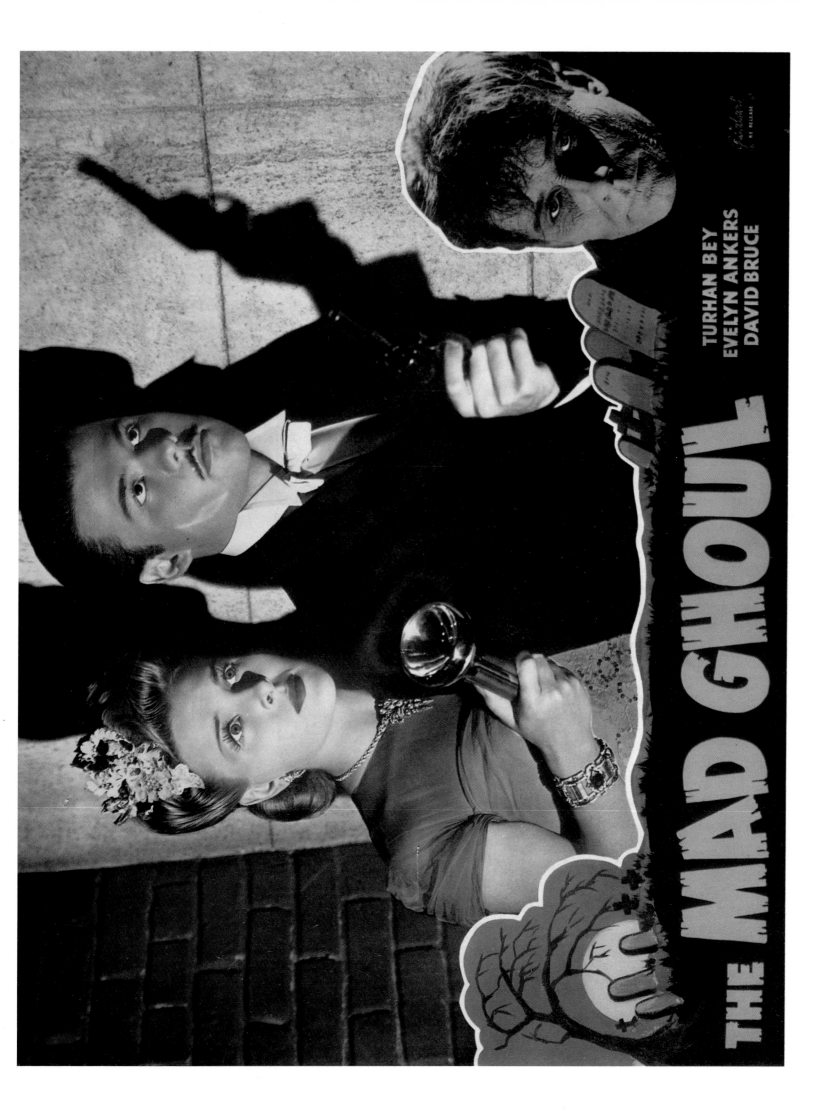

The Mad Ghoul

1943 Universal Pictures
Producer Ben Pivar
Director James P. Hogan
Story Hans Kraly
Screenplay Brenda Weisberg,
Paul Gangelin
Camera Milton Krasner
Special Effects John P. Fulton
Art Director John B. Goodman
Editor Milton Carruth
Music Charles Previn
Musical Director Hans J. Salter
Makeup Jack P. Pierce
65 minutes

David Bruce *Ted Allison*
Evelyn Ankers *Isobel Lewis*
George Zucco *Dr Alfred Morris*
Robert Armstrong *Ken McClure*
Turhan Bey *Eric Iverson*
Milburn Stone *Sgt Macklin*
Rose Heart *Della*
Addison Richards *Gavigan*
Charles McGraw *Garrity*
Gus Glassmire *Caretaker*
Andrew Toombes

'Monster of Murder!' screamed the publicity material. 'Lips of Ice! Craving Flesh! Eyes of Fire Demanding Love!' it continued, getting a second wind. 'Cadaverous Claws! Death-masked Face!' it added, finally concluding with the immortal phrase, 'Heart a Throbbing Tomb of Hate!' I can scarcely continue. George Zucco, he of the eyes like polished marbles, played a college professor who discovers the formula for a curious gas used by the ancient Egyptians to cause a state of 'Death in Life'. Naturally he must experiment on his star pupil, David Bruce, and a whiff or three soon changes him into a haggard zombie, a slave to Zucco's commands. These include a few murders made necessary by the antidote to zombiedom, extract of newly killed human heart. Zucco is madly in love with Evelyn Ankers, as which red-blooded fan of Forties B-movies was not. Our Evelyn, known at the time as Queen of the B's, is a concert singer who travels around warbling 'I Dreamt I Dwelt in Marble Halls', courtesy of a Miss Lillian Cornell, who graciously lent her her voice. Complications ensue when Zucco learns Evelyn loves her pianist, the dashingly oriental Turhan Bey. The only thing to do is send in David Bruce. Doing always whatever he is bid, the zombified Bruce clambers up on to the stage in the middle of Evelyn's, or Lillian's, top note, determined to shoot the pianist. All ends happily, however, with Doctor Zucco, gassed into a zombie, clawing desperately at a nearby grave in search of a heart. 'Piffling Lyceum!' was the verdict of the *Kinematograph Weekly*.

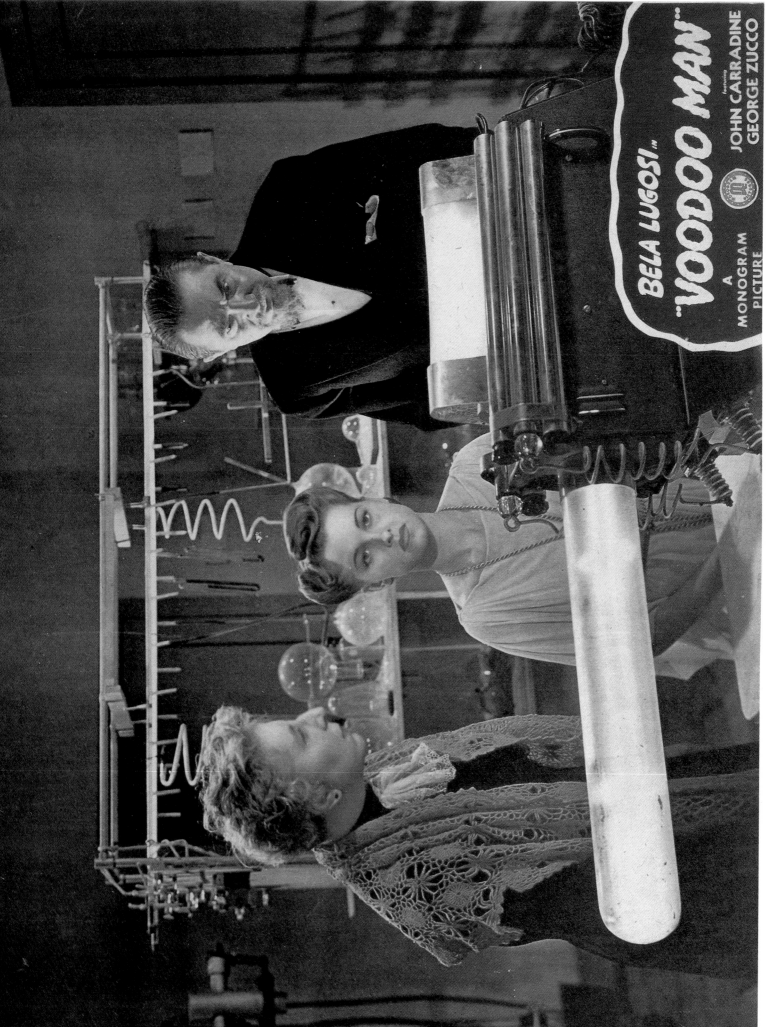

Voodoo Man

1944 Banner Pictures
Distributor Monogram Pictures
Producer Sam Katzman, Jack Dietz
Associate Producer Barney A. Sarecky
Director William Beaudine
Screenplay Robert Charles
Camera Marcel le Picard
Art Director David Milton
Editor Carl Pierson
Music Edward J. Kay
62 minutes

Bela Lugosi *Dr Marlowe*
John Carrdine *Job*
George Zucco *Nicholas*
Michael Ames *Ralph Davison*
Wanda McKay *Betty Benton*
Ellen Hall *Evelyn Marlowe*
Lousie Currie *Stella Saunders*
Henry Hall *Sheriff*
Dan White *Deputy*
Mary Currier *Mrs Benton*
Pat McKee *Grego*
Claire James *Zombie*
Terry Walker *Alice*
Mici Goetz *Marie*

Beware – the Return of the Katzman! Here comes Sam, the favourite producer of grade B movie macabre, this time uniting that terrible trio of the bottom of the bill, Bela Lugosi, John Carradine and George Zucco. Bela tops as Dr Marlowe, a curiously English name for a Transylvanian. Perhaps the story was written for Boris Karloff? Marlowe has a pretty young wife, but only because she has been preserved as a zombie for the last twenty years. In his never-ending search for a way to revive her, Lugosi employs a loping dope called Job, played by John Carradine with his hair down. Once a girl is kidnapped, Lugosi and his chum, George Zucco, don strange robes and start chanting in the hope that voodoo will transfer the girl's life force to the zombie. Each experiment fails, and the consequently zombified girl joins the cast of previous victims locked away in Job's cellar. 'Hmmm!' hums Job as he strokes a victim's hair, 'You're a pretty one!'

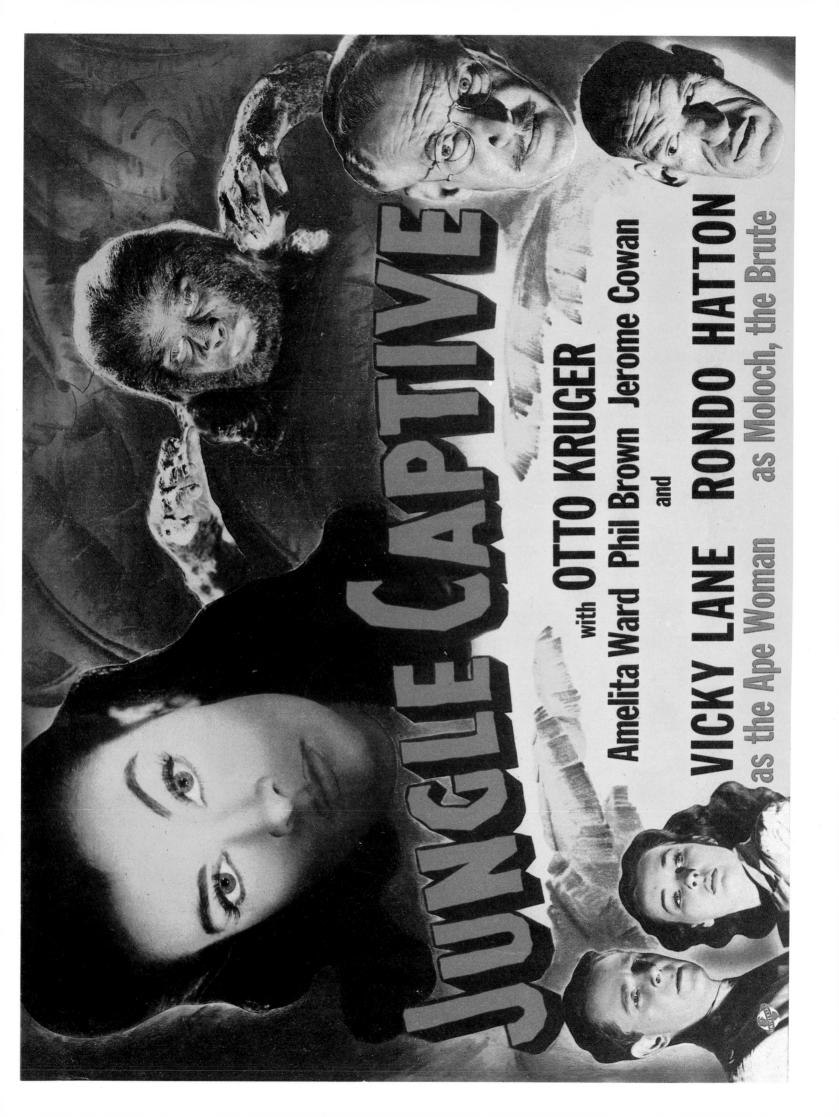

Jungle Captive

Reissue title Wild Jungle Captive
1945 Universal Pictures
Executive Producer Ben Pivar
Associate Producer Morgan B. Cox
Director Harold Young
Story Dwight V. Babcock
Screenplay Dwight V. Babcock,
       M. Coates Webster
Camera Maury Gertsman
Special Effects John P. Fulton
Editor Fred Feitshans Jr
Art Director John B. Goodman
Music Paul Sawtell
Makeup Jack P. Pierce
64 minutes

Otto Kruger *Dr Stendhal*
Amelita Ward *Ann Forrester*
Phil Brown *Don Young*
Vicky Lane *Paula Dupree*
Rondo Hatton *Moloch*
Jerome Cowan *Insp Harrigan*
Eddie Acuff *Bill*
Charles Wagenheim *Fred*
Ernie Adams *Jim*
Jack Overman *Detective*
Eddy Chandler *Motor-cyclist*

Dr Stendhal, of the Stendhal Biological Laboratories (Electrolytic Research), 413 Old Orchard Road, is a brilliant but unstable biochemist. Of course. He is played by Otto Kruger. Having perfected a method of resuscitating dead rabbits, he determines to experiment on the corpse of the late Paula Dupree, a lady who has passed on in the shape of an ape (vide *Jungle Woman*, same studio, previous year). He sends his handyman, known on all lobby cards as Moloch the Brute, down to the local mortuary to fetch Paula's corpse, a simple task which takes but the murder of the morgue attendant. Hefting the ape back to the lab, Moloch assists while Stendhal injects it with the blood of a girl. Both seem somewhat surprised when the ape's body changes into that of pretty Vicky Lane. (After all, Paula Dupree had previously been played by the sultry Acquanetta.) Diagnosing that Vicky is mentally subnormal, Stendhal comes up with the perfect solution. A brain transplant! He has one to hand, well almost – that of his young and intelligent secretary, Amelita Ward. Scalpels are akimbo when the ape-woman suddenly becomes an all-ape again and strangles both the doctor and poor old Moloch. Then the cops arrive and mow down the ape, ending a three-picture series before there can be a fourth.

BORIS KARLOFF

in ROBERT LOUIS STEVENSON'S

THE BODY SNATCHER

45/85

The Body Snatcher

1945 RKO Radio Pictures

Executive Producer Jack J. Gross
Producer Val Lewton
Director Robert Wise
Story from the short story by
 Robert Louis Stevenson
Screenplay Philip MacDonald,
 Val Lewton (as Carlos Keith)
Camera Robert De Grasse
Editor J.R. Whittredge
Art Director Albert S. D'Agostino
Music Roy Webb
Musical Director Constantin Bakeleinikoff
Assistant Director Harry Scott
64 minutes

Boris Karloff *John Grey*
Bela Lugosi *Joseph*
Henry Daniell *Dr Toddy MacFarlane*
Edith Atwater *Meg Camden*
Russell Wade *Donald Fettes*
Rita Corday *Mrs Marsh*
Sharyn Moffett *Georgina Marsh*
Donna Lee *Street Singer*
Robert Clarke *Richardson*
Carl Kent *Gilchrist*
Jack Welch *Boy*
Larry Wheat *Salesman*
Mary Gordon *Mary McBride*
Jim Moran *Trader*
Ina Constant *Maid*

The two greatest names in horror film stardom were teamed in this wartime B-picture. A least, according to the advertising they were. But while Karloff carried the film to its impressive heights as one of the minor classics of the genre, Lugosi's part was really a minor support, being choked off by his old Universal oppo early on in the proceedings. Robert Louis Stevenson, the Victorian Scots author of the still chilling *Dr Jekyll and Mr Hyde*, based his tale on the near-legendary misdemeanours of Messrs Burke and Hare, body-snatchers to the trade. Karloff is the sinister coachman in Edinburgh, 1831, who finds a less tiring way of supplying surgeons with fresh cadavers than robbing newly-dug graves. A nice quiet quick kill, and presto! Another warm body for the scalpel. Brilliantly supported by the usually fey Henry Daniell, Karloff is finally done away with, then returns in a terrifying climax, riding a lightning storm beside Daniell in his rickety carriage – a chill missed by those Britishers who first saw the film on its original release. The censor cut it out!

"THE VAMPIRE'S GHOST"

featuring

JOHN ABBOTT · CHARLES GORDON

with

PEGGY STEWART · GRANT WITHERS · ADELE MARA

LESLEY SELANDER – *Director*

Screen Play
JOHN K. BUTLER *and* **LEIGH BRACKETT**

Original Story – **LEIGH BRACKETT**

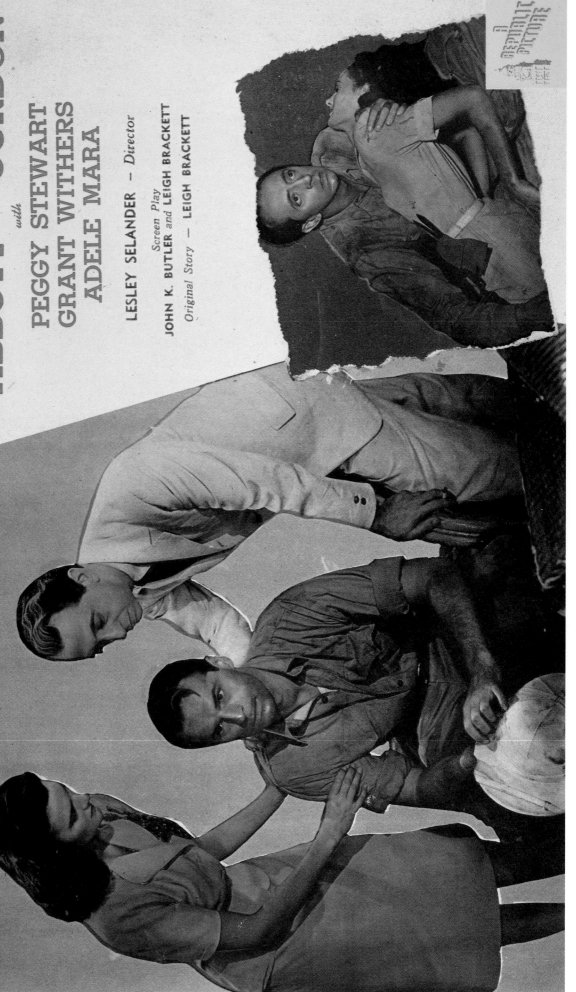

The Vampire's Ghost

1945 Republic Pictures
Producer Herbert J. Yates
Associate Producer Rudolph E. Abel
Director Lesley Selander
Story Leigh Brackett
Screenplay Leigh Brackett, John K. Butler
Camera Bud Thackery
Special Effects Howard and Theodore Lydecker
Editor Tony Martinelli
Art Director Russell Kimball
Music Richard Cherwin
Choreographer Jerry Jarrette
59 minutes

John Abbott Webb Fallon
Charles Gordon Roy Hendrick
Peggy Stewart Julie Vance
Grant Withers Father Gilchrist
Adele Mara Lisa
Emmett Vogan Thomas Vance
Roy Barcroft Jim Barratt
Martin Wilkins Simon Peter
Frank Jacquet Doctor
Jimmy Aubrey Bum

English actors were always considered ideal for menacing roles in the old Hollywood. Boris Karloff himself, George Zucco, Henry Daniell, Basil Rathbone, the list goes on and on. Especially if you would usually find John Abbott lurking. Republic Pictures, that home of the B-western, had a go at promoting Abbott to wartime stardom in such minor mysteries as *The London Blackout Murders*. Here he is as a full-blooded (when he can get it) vampire, able to shatter a mirror at a single bloodshot glance. The setting for this batwing-ding is, of all places, the West Coast of Africa, and popular heavy Grant Withers plays the good Catholic Father bound to hound him down. On the surface Abbott plays the local king of the underworld, but once exposed as the supernatural fiend who has been hanging around under a curse since the days of Good Queen Bess, he abducts the heroine and is all set to burn her alive at the stake. This is where Father Grant Withers comes in handy with a crucifix. Directed by Lesley Selander, usually to be found lensing Hopalong Cassidy westerns, the film is mainly notable for its bar-room brawls.

MONOGRAM PICTURES presents "THE FACE of MARBLE"

Face of Marble

1946 Monogram Pictures
Producer Jeffrey Bernerd
Director William Beaudine
Story William Thiele, Edmund Hartmann
Screenplay Michel Jacoby
Camera Harry Neumann
Special Effects Robert Clarke
Editor William Austin
Art Director David Milton
Music Edward Kay
70 minutes

John Carradine *Prof Randolph*
Claudia Drake *Elaine Randolph*
Robert Shayne *Dr David Cochran*
Maris Wrixon *Linda*
Thomas E. Jackson *Insp Norton*
Willie Best *Shadrach*
Rosa Rey *Marika*
Neil Burns *Jeff*
Donald Kerr *Photographer*
Allan Ray *Photographer*
General the Dog *Brutus*

Professor Randolph is a brilliant but unbalanced scientist, a foregone conclusion thanks to the casting of John Carradine. He thinks he can restore life to the asphyxiated by means of electricity, a decent enough theory, and tries out his methods on a handy drowned sailor. The seaman revives, but in a whitened state of half-life, half-death. He promptly goes berserk and dies in a wreckage of laboratory machinery. This fails to faze the prof, who continues his experiments, this time on his Great Dane, Brutus. The dog is killed, then restored to life. Crazed and whitened, the beast walks through a window without breaking the glass! Meanwhile, Marika, the Haitian housekeeper, tries a spot of local voodoo on the professor's assistant, who she thinks is in love with the professor's fiancee. This fails, so she decides to murder the assistant's fiancee. She kills the professor's wife by mistake. The professor then decides to restore his dead wife to life. Deranged and whitened, she kills her husband. Marika commits suicide, and zombie wife and zombie dog walk into the sea, leaving the young doctor and his fiancee to ponder on the shore. *Film Report* had this to say: 'This wildly fantastic and ludicrous story is so extravagant that even the most unsophisticated are unlikely to take it seriously'. The verdict still holds.

The Catman of Paris

A TWIN FEATURE RE-PRESENTATION

The Catman of Paris

1946 Republic Pictures
Producer Herbert J. Yates
Associate Producer Marek M. Libkov
Director Lesley Selander
Screenplay Sherman L. Lowe
Camera Reggie Lanning
Special Effects Howard and Theodore
Lydecker
Art Director Gano Chittenden
Editor Harry Keller
Music Dale Butts
Musical Director Richard Cherwin
Choreographer Larry Cebalos
Makeup Bob Mark
65 minutes

Carl Esmond *Charles Regouer*
Lenore Aubert *Marie Audet*
Douglas Dumbrille *Bouchard*
Gerald Mohr *Insp Severin*
Fritz Feld *Prefect*
Francis Pierlot *Renier*
George Renavent *Audet*
Francis McDonald
Maurice Cass
Adele Mara
John Dehner
Anthony Caruso
Robert J. Wilke *The Catman*

Unshown in the UK for fear of being branded with the dread 'H', the Board of Censors Certificate which prevented all persons under the age of sixteen from being contaminated by horrific pictures, this pocket-sized production from the famous Poverty Row producers, Republic, grew a reputation beyond its lower-bracket worth. Directed by king of the cow-operas, Lesley Selander, and scripted by one of Republic's regular serial scribes, Sherman L. Lowe, when the film was finally seen at the Gothique Film Society of London, it was exposed as a fairly confusing example of B-cinema supernatural. Set in the Paris of 1896, Carl Esmond plays a brilliant young author fresh back from travels in the Orient. This has given him a touch of the mental blackouts and when he revives from same it looks as if he is the hirsute, clawed creature who is going around killing off women – the Catman, as the Parisian press has branded him. Lenore Aubert, lovely daughter of Esmond's posh publisher, is convinced that Carl is nothing of the suchwhich, although Gerald Mohr, Inspector of the Sureté, thinks otherwise. Who does it turn out to be? Suffice to say it is not really the actor it appears to be, because a special effect by Howard and Theodore Lydecker turns him into another actor at these critical and star-crossed moments. Released in America on a double-bill with *Valley of the Zombies*. Hence the double lobby card.

GOLDEN GATE PICTURES, Presents

Scared to Death

STARRING

BELA LUGOSI · GEORGE ZUCCO

NAT PENDLETON · MOLLY LAMONT

DISTRIBUTED BY SCREEN GUILD PRODUCTIONS,

PHOTOGRAPHED IN

Full Natural COLOR

Scared to Death

1946 Golden Gate Pictures
Distributor Screen Guild
Producer William B. David
Director Christy Cabanne
Screenplay W. J. Abbott
Camera Marcel le Picard
Art Director Harry Reif
Editor George McGuire
Music Carl Hoefle
Makeup Roland Ray
65 minutes Cinecolor

Bela Lugosi *Prof Leonide*
George Zucco *Doctor Van Ec*
Nat Pendleton *Bill*
Molly Lamont *Laura Van Ec*
Douglas Fowley *Terry Lee*
Joyce Compton *Jane Cornell*
Roland Varno *Bill Raymond*
Gladys Blake *Lilybeth*
Lee Bennett *Rene*
Angelo Rossito *Indigo*

This tale of terror told by a woman's corpse – she has been literally scared to death as per title – marks the grave of the true B-picture horror. After 1946 the Hollywood system changed considerably, and major studios stopped manufacturing lower-case padding for double bills, leaving it to very minor production companies who seldom could afford a permanent address, even on Poverty Row. It was also the first minor horror film to sport colour, and while the lobby cards billed it as 'Full Natural Color', the screen gave credit to Cinecolor, that poor man's process which sometimes tinted the odd B-western. Bela Lugosi and George Zucco teamed again, for the first time in colour, as a stage magician and a sinister doctor. Lugosi is assisted by a very small dwarf, Angelo Rossito, who frequently accompanied the old vampire on his stage shows. Zucco portrays a dead doctor who returns as a phoney walking corpse in order to frighten his wife into her coffin. He succeeds, despite Lugosi and his hypnosis, and the film ends unhappily for all, including comic relief Nat Pendleton.

J. FRANCIS WHITE and JOY N. HOUCK present

LOST WOMEN

STARRING

JACKIE COOGAN · RICHARD TRAVIS
ALLAN NIXON · LYLE TALBOT

CO-STARRING MARY HILL and ROBERT KNAPP

INTRODUCING TANDRA QUINN (THE TARANTULA GIRL)

WITH

CHRIS PIN MARTIN and SAMUEL WU

Directed by HERBERT TEVOS and RON ORMOND

Produced by MELVIN GORDON and WILLIAM PERKINS

A HOWCO PRODUCTION

Lost Women

1952 Howco Productions
Executive Producers J. Francis White,
Joy N. Houck
Producers Melvin Gordon,
William Perkins
Directors Herbert Tevos, Ron Ormond
Screenplay Herbert Tevos
Photography Gil Warrenton, Karl Struss
Music Hoyt Curtin
Editors Donn Keyes, Hugh Winn,
Ray Lockert
Special Effects Ray Mercer
69 minutes

Jackie Coogan *Dr Aranya*
Allan Nixon *Doc Tucker*
Richard Travis *Dan Mulcahey*
Tandra Quinn *Tarantella*
Lyle Talbot *Narrator*
Mary Hill *Doreen*
Robert Knapp *Grant Phillips*
Chris-Pin Martin *Pepe*
Harmon Stevens *Masterson*
Nico Lek *Jan Van Croft*
Samuel Wu *Wu*
George Barrows *George*
John Martin *Charley*

Originally made as *Mesa of Lost Women*, and later known as *Lost Women of Zarpa*, this is the B-horror that couldn't make up its mind: is it the worst B-horror ever made or not? The lobby cards aren't letting on, with their boast that this is the film that 'Introduces Tandra Quinn as the Tarantula Girl' and the *Aurum Encyclopedia of Horror* lets readers make up their own mind by ignoring the film altogether. *Variety*, the American 'showman's bible', decided that 'the picture obviously was made on the premise that product-hungry theatres would be forced to book anything'. Plot apart, the most curious thing about the picture is that it was chosen as a comeback role for a former child star of silent screen comedies, Jackie Coogan, who since his days as the knee-high, winsome Kid has grown into a bald and baleful bloke, best known for his sexy marriages. Here he plays a bespectacled scientist, insane of course, who has a laboratory buried in the Mexican desert. He spends his time creating monsters out of tarantula spiders to guard his domain, while infusing a bevy of beauties with their savage essence. One of them, Tarantella the Tarantula Girl, of course, executes a curious Spider Dance in the local cantina before the explosive climax.

House of Wax

1953 Warner Brothers
Producer Bryan Foy
Director Andre de Toth
Story from the play *Waxworks*
   by Charles Belden
Screenplay Crane Wilbur
Photography Bert Glennon,
   Peverell Marley
Editor Rudi Fehr
Art Director Stanley Fleischer
Natural Vision Supervisor M.L. Gunsburg
Music David Buttolph
88 minutes Warnercolor Stereoscopic

Vincent Price *Prof Jarrod*
Frank Lovejoy *Lt Brennan*
Phyllis Kirk *Sue Allen*
Carolyn Jones *Cathy Grey*
Paul Picerni *Scott Andrews*
Roy Roberts *Matthew Burke*
Angela Clarke *Mrs Andrews*
Paul Cavanaugh *Sidney Wallace*
Charles Buchinsky *Igor*
Ned Young *Leon Averill*
Dabbs Greer *Sgt Shane*
Philip Tonge

The chances are slight that you will ever see this superior horror film in the way it was originally intended. It was made in 'Natural Vision', a stereoscopic process involving two cameras, one for the left eye, one for the right, and therefore two projectors. And also, of course, to be seen through polaroid spectacles, articles not easy to come by these days, almost forty years on from its preview. Thus the stereoscopic visual effects, including the wiggling bottoms of the can-can girls, are seen but not appreciated in the flat versions shown on television. Actually, they were not seen and therefore unappreciated in the UK, whose censors, despite awarding the film with an 'X' for adults as well as an 'H' for horror, snipped out these offensive sequences in a misguided attempt to keep British eyeballs clean. Equally, the stereophonic score in Warnerphonic Sound also disappeared with the passing years, so the bump behind you when a chair is chucked out of the screen no longer shocks. This is the film credited with the rebirth of Vincent Price as everybody's favourite horror hero. He appears as the devoted waxwork modeller, mutilated and maddened after the fire set by his business partner when their Wax Museum literally goes into the red. Wearing a wax mask to hide his horribly disfigured features, Price bowls about in a wheelchair, coating corpses with molten wax and moulding them into figures of history. Before pretty Phyllis Kirk can be plunged into a wax bath, she is plucked to safety by the sculptor who loves her for what she is – alive. A remake of Warner's famous Thirties horror flick, *The Mystery of the Wax Museum*, this does better by setting the story back in 1900, but worse by having a much less horrific smashing of the madman's wax face by the heroine. Incidentally, not everybody was privileged to see the film in 3-D: note the patch on the lobby card covering the Three Dimension announcement.

REVENGE OF THE CREATURE

Starring

JOHN AGAR
LORI NELSON
JOHN BROMFIELD

with **NESTOR PAIVA**

Directed by JACK ARNOLD
Screenplay by MARTIN BERKELEY
Produced by WILLIAM ALLAND

A UNIVERSAL-INTERNATIONAL PICTURE

Revenge of the Creature

1955 Universal International
Producer William Alland
Director Jack Arnold
Screenplay Martin Berkeley
Story based on characters in
The Creature from the Black Lagoon
by Arthur Ross and Harry Essex
Camera Charles Welbourne
Art Director Alexander Golitzen
Editor Paul Weatherwax
Music Joseph Gershenson
Makeup Bud Westmore
82 minutes Stereoscopic

John Agar *Clete Ferguson*
Lori Nelson *Helen Dobson*
John Bromfield *Joe Hayes*
Nestor Paiva *Lucas*
Robert Williams *Geroge Johnson*
Grandon Rhodes *Foster*
Dave Willock *Gibson*
Charles Cane *Captain*
Ricou Browning *Creature (water)*
Don Megowan *Creature (land)*

The sex appeal of monster movies was seldom better demonstrated than in the first two of the three Gill-Man movies, beginning in 1954's *Creature from the Black Lagoon* with the Gill-Man floating beneath the dark waters as Julia Adams, in her white one-piece bathing suit, swam curvaceously above him. In this film it is Lori Nelson, cast for her form in a swimsuit, who lures the finny fellow out of his depths. Messrs Bromfield and Williams trap the beast and transport him from his Amazon home to a Florida Oceanarium, where John Agar, he-man and ichthyologist, tries to teach him to speak. The Gill-Man's lust for Lori finally makes him break his chains and carry her off, intent, one supposes, to drown her in his Black Lagoon. Agar and the cops put an end to his plan, and riddled with bullets he goes down in the water, but not for the last time. Next year he returned in *The Creature Walks Among Us*. Although made in three dimensions, this film was only shown in two, as far as the UK was concerned.

CULT OF THE COBRA

STARRING

FAITH DOMERGUE
RICHARD LONG
MARSHALL THOMPSON
KATHLEEN HUGHES

with **WILLIAM REYNOLDS**
JACK KELLY
MYRNA HANSEN
DAVID JANSSEN

Directed by FRANCIS D. LYON
Screenplay by JERRY DAVIS,
CECIL MAIDEN and RICHARD COLLINS
Produced by HOWARD PINE

A UNIVERSAL-INTERNATIONAL PICTURE

Cult of the Cobra

1955 Universal International

Producer Howard Pine
Director Francis D. Lyon
Screenplay Jerry Davis, Cecil Maiden,
 Richard Collins
Photography Russel Metty
Art Director Alexander Golitzen
Editor Milton Carruth
Music Joseph Gershenson
79 minutes

Faith Domergue *Lisa Moya*
Richard Long *Paul Able*
Marshall Thompson *Tom Markel*
Kathleen Hughes *Julia*
William Reynolds *Pete Norton*
Jack Kelly *Carl Turner*
Myrna Hansen *Marian*
David Janssen *Rico Nardi*
James Dobson *Nick Hommel*
Leonard Strong *Daru*
Walter Coy *Inspector*

What happens when six brash young GIs stationed in India smuggle themselves into the temple of a secret cult of snake worshippers? These locals believe that they can change themselves into cobras and back to normal at will. How silly! And yet . . . The soldiers are discovered and cursed by the High Priest, who declares they will all die at the hands, or perhaps forked tongue, of the Snake Goddess. As the men are about to fly back to the States for separation from the service, one of them dies in mysterious circumstances. Back in New York, Marshall Thompson meets Faith Domergue, an exotic lady with a slight lisp who lives in the apartment opposite. Then one by one, three more of the buddies are killed. Thompson is naturally sceptical when Richard Long suspects that Miss Domergue belongs to the Indian cult and is responsible for the killings, but less so when he finds Kathleen Hughes in her dressing-room under threat from a large cobra. And even less so when, having slung the snake out of her window, Thompson sees the dead body of Domergue lying on the pavement below. A film that sounds better than it actually was, thanks to the smallness of the snake and the largeness of Faith Domergue.

Tarantula

1955 Universal International
Producer William Alland
Director Jack Arnold
Story Jack Arnold, Robert Fresco
Screenplay Robert Fresco,
                Martin Berkeley
Camera George Robinson
Special Effects Clifford Stine
Editor William Morgan
Art Director Alexander Golitzen
Music Joseph Gershenson
Makeup Bud Westmore
80 minutes

John Agar *Dr Matt Hastings*
Mara Corday *Stephanie Clayton*
Leo G. Carroll *Prof Deemer*
Nestor Paiva *Sheriff Andrews*
Ross Elliott *Joe Burch*
Edwin Rand *Lt John Nolan*
Raymond Bailey *Townsend*
Hank Patterson *Josh*
Bert Holland *Barney Russell*
Steve Darrell *Andy Anderson*

John Agar, fast becoming a favourite with fantasy film-makers thanks to his cheerful acceptance of any role that came his way, played a husky research scientist in this monstrous merry-go-round which coupled a popular theme of the Fifties, outsize spiders, with that throwback to the Forties, acromegaly (*The Monster Maker*, *The Brute Man*, etc). We find him labouring in a lonely shack at Desert Rock, Arizona, doing his best to develop an Automatically Stabilized Nutrient Formula that will nourish the world's expanding population when natural supplies run out. Assisted by that well-loved combination of scientific intelligence and physical beauty, Mara Corday, he investigates a fire in the lab. An outsize tarantula, injected with the unstable stuff, escapes and is soon terrorising the landscape, eating whole cows as it expands in size, finally returning to tower over the entire two-storey laboratory. To make matters worse, old Leo G. Carroll, not the most handsome of men to start with, has injected himself and changed into a lumpish obscenity. The spider stomps the lab into the dust and heads for the desert, where it takes the entire local leg of the United States Air Force to burn it to ash with napalm.

SCIENTISTS TURN MEN INTO BEASTS!

ADULT ENTERTAINMENT

CLASSIFIED BY ONTARIO BOARD OF CENSORS AS

THE WEREWOLF

with DON MEGOWAN · JOYCE HOLDEN

introducing STEVEN RITCH as THE WEREWOLF

Story and Screen Play by ROBERT E. KENT and JAMES B. GORDON · Produced by SAM KATZMAN · Directed by FRED F. SEARS · A CLOVER PRODUCTION · A COLUMBIA PICTURE

The Werewolf

1956 Clover Productions
Distributor Columbia Pictures
Producer Sam Katzman
Director Fred F. Sears
Screenplay Robert E. Kent,
    James B. Gordon
Camera Edward Linden
Editor Harold White
Art Director Paul Palmentola
Music Mischa Bakeleinikoff
79 minutes

Steven Ritch *Duncan March*
Don Megowan *Jack Haines*
Joyce Holden *Amy Standish*
Eleanore Tanin *Helen Marsh*
Kim Charney *Chris Marsh*
Harry Lauter *Clovey*
Larry Blake *Dirgus*
Ken Christy *Dr James Gilchrist*
James Gavin *Fanning*
John Launer *Dr Emery Forrest*
George Lynn *Dr Morgan Chambers*
George Cisar *Hoxie*
Don Harvey *Deputy*

Sam Katzman, the producer with a finger on the public pulse and a tight hand on the private purse, switched his affection from B-horrors to B-sci-fi with this picture, which combined them both in whichever order you prefer. It took the ever-popular theme of the legendary werewolf and force-married it to the trendy genre of super-science. 'Scientists Turn Men Into Beasts!' explained the lobby cards at the top of their voice, while the Ontario Board of Film Censors spoiled the artwork by plastering it with an 'Adults Only' warning. A pair of experimenting scientists, Doctors Gilchrist and Forrest, come across the victim of an auto accident. He seems an ideal subject for their serum which is intended to save mankind from atomic radiation, so they inject him. Unfortunately it turns him into a werewolf, and he rips the throat out of a small-town hold-up man, subsequently changing back into decent Steven Ritch. His periodic changes to wolf under stress upsets his wife and son, who eventually help the local lawman track him down and shoot him. Sad.

A BLOOD-SUCKING MUMMY...A SEDUCTIVE CAT-GODDESS...

—Unleashing 4,000 Years of Horror Upon This Century!

PHARAOH'S CURSE

STARRING

MARK DANA · ZIVA SHAPIR

DIANE BREWSTER

with GEORGE NEISE · ALVARA GUILLOT

BEN WRIGHT

Original Story and Screenplay by
RICHARD LANDAU

Music by
LES BAXTER

Produced by
HOWARD W. KOCH

Directed by
LEE SHOLEM

Executive Producer
AUBREY SCHENCK

A BEL-AIR PRODUCTION

RELEASED THRU
UNITED ARTISTS

Pharaoh's Curse

1956 Bel Air Productions
Distributor United Artists
Executive Producer Aubrey Schenck
Producer Howard W. Koch
Director Lee Sholem
Screenplay Richard Landau
Camera William Margulies
Music Les Baxter
Editor George Gittens
Art Director Bob Kinoshita
66 minutes

Mark Dana *Captain Storm*
Ziva Shapir *Simira*
Diane Brewster *Sylvia Quentin*
George Neise *Robert Quentin*
Alvara Guillot *Numar*
Ben Wright *Walter Andrews*
Terence De Marney *Sgt Smollett*
Ralph Clanton
Kurt Katch
Guy Prescott *Dr Michael Faraday*

Fanatical George Neise is to blame for the monstrous goings-on in this minor movie. He heads an archaeolgical expedition up the Nile and into the Valley of the Kings, despite the warnings of a mysterious Arab girl. Do not desecrate the tomb of a royal Egyptian Priest, she warns, having seen earlier Hollywood B-movies on the same theme. Ignoring the sense of this, Neise opens up the sacred sarcophagus and lo, therein lies a mummy. A swift incision into its wrappings and an unexpected thing happens. The spirit of the brother of the Arab girl is sucked inside the bandaged corpse, thanks to an ancient curse, thus bringing the remains of the old one back to life, and, quote, 'Unleashing Four Thousand Years of Horror upon This Century!' Stomping about, sucking the blood of the infidel hither and yon, crumbling into pieces as it goes, the mummy is ultimately sealed into the tomb by falling rocks. George Neise goes with him. But how did respected English stage actor Terence De Marney get mixed up in this?

TERROR ON THE AFRICAN VOODOO COAST!

ZOMBIES OF MORA TAU

GREGG ALLISON AUTUMN
PALMER · HAYES · RUSSELL

with

Screen Play by RAYMOND T. MARCUS · Story by GEORGE PLYMPTON
Produced by SAM KATZMAN · Directed by EDWARD CAHN
A CLOVER PRODUCTION · A COLUMBIA PICTURE

Zombies of Mora-Tau

UK title The Dead That Walk
1957 Clover Productions
Distributor Columbia Pictures
Producer Sam Katzman
Director Edward L. Cahn
Story George H. Plympton
Screenplay Raymond T. Marcus
Camera Benjamin H. Kline
Art Director Paul Palmentola
Editor Jack Ogilvie
Music Mischa Bakeleinikoff
71 minutes

George Palmer *Jeff Clark*
Allison Hayes *Mona Harrison*
Autumn Russell *Jan*
Joel Ashley *George Harrison*
Morris Ankrum *Jonathan Eggert*
Marjorie Eaton *Mrs Peters*
Gene Roth *Sam*
Leonard Geer *Johnnie*

Columbia Pictures were so embarrassed by this Sam Katzman B-picture, that in the UK they gave it to little Eros Films to release. Eros promptly changed its silly name, knowing their new title would at least appeal to their customers who still loved the old Forties frighteners. George Harrison (you can tell it's an old movie when they give the hero a name like that!) and his wife, Mona, intend to salvage a treasure of rough diamonds from a sunken wreck off the African Coast – 'The African Vodoo Coast' as the lobby cards put it. They hire Jeff Clark as their diver, and are given shelter by the lovely Jan's aged grandmother, Mrs Peters. This crone is against their intent as her husband, possibly her late husband, is one of the walking corpses who grope about the deeps guarding the treasure. Mona is murdered by the amphibious zombies and becomes a zombie herself, and is actually the one to kill her husband. Meanwhile Jeff dives for the diamonds, but bends an ear to Mrs Peters' pleas that he return the gems to the seas. When he does so, the ancient curse is lifted and the zombie guards dissolve away to eternal rest.

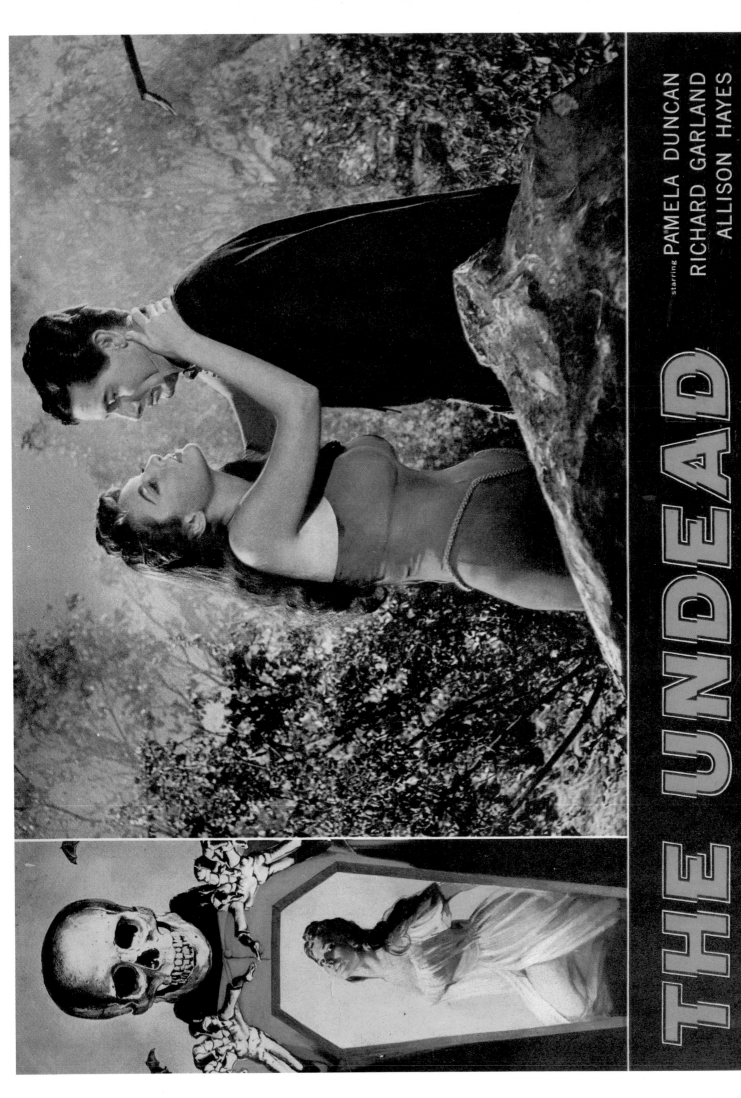

THE UNDEAD

starring PAMELA DUNCAN · RICHARD GARLAND · ALLISON HAYES

with VAL DUFOUR · MEL WELLES · Produced and Directed by ROGER CORMAN · Screenplay by CHARLES GRIFFITH & MARK HANNA · An AMERICAN-INTERNATIONAL Picture

The Undead

1957 Balboa Productions
Distributor American International
Producer Roger Corman
Director Roger Corman
Screenplay Charles Griffith,
Mark Hanna
Camera William Sickner
Editor Frank Sullivan
Music Ronald Stein
71 minutes

Pamela Duncan *Helene/Diane*
Richard Garland *Pendragon*
Allison Hayes *Livia*
Val Dufour *Quintus*
Mel Welles *Smolkin*
Dorothy Neuman *Mag Maud*
Billy Barty *Imp*
Bruno Ve Sota *Scroop*
Richard Devon *Satan*
Aaron Saxon *Gobbo*

This fogbound film was a typical Roger Corman quickie shot in an abandoned supermarket on Sunset Boulevard in an attempt to cash in on the contemporary craze for reincarnation by hypnosis inspired by the best-selling book, *The Search for Bridey Murphy*. Pamela Duncan starred as a call-girl regressed by a psychiatrist, Dr Quinton, to her ancestress who was burned as a witch in medieval times. As a witness to these historic events, she tries to interfere with history to save herself from the bonfire. Unfortunately she comes up against the power of Allison Hayes, who is in league with Satan himself (Richard Devon) via her half-pint familiar, played by Hollywood's favourite midget, Billy Barty. The doctor finally realises that if he allows her to save herself, the whole path of history will be altered and he will thus lose a paying patient. He tries a spot of self-mesmerism, returns to the past, and gets trapped in time. This complicated picture failed to gain distribution in the UK except as an 8-millimetre home movie. Cut down to sixteen minutes it made even less sense than it did before.

LURED! – to the HOUSE OF MONSTERS.....

Guaranteed to FRIGHTEN!

NO ESCAPE FROM

THE UNEARTHLY

Starring JOHN CARRADINE · ALLISON HAYES · MYRON HEALY

with SALLY TODD · MARILYN BUFERD · TOR JOHNSON · Original Story by JANE MANN · Screen Play by JANE MANN · Screen Play by GEOFFREY DENNIS and JANE MANN

Produced and Directed by BROOKE L. PETERS · An AB-PT Picture · Distributed by Republic Pictures Corporation

The Unearthly

1957 A.B.–P.T. Pictures
Distributor Republic Pictures
Producer Brooke L. Peters
Director Brooke L. Peters
Story Jane Mann
Screenplay Geoffrey Dennis,
    Jane Mann
Camera Merle Connell
Editor Richard Currier
Art Director Daniel Hall
Music Henry Varse
73 (68) minutes

John Carradine *Prof Charles Conway*
Allison Hayes *Grace Thomas*
Myron Healy *Mark Houston*
Sally Todd *Natalie*
Marilyn Buferd *Dr Gilchrist*
Tor Johnson *Lobo*
Arthur Batanides *Danny Green*
Harry Fleer *Jedrow*
Roy Gordon

Lean, mean John Carradine played Professor Charles Conway, mad scientist, in this monstrous melodrama of mixed-up mutations. He and his pretty assistant, Dr Gilchrist, have a secret laboratory in their remote mansion in darkest Georgia, where they hope to discover the secret of eternal life. All they have to show for it so far is a cellarful of deformed creatures, no two alike thanks to the miracle of makeup. These things, ever raving and waving, are guarded by a half-witted hulk called Lobo, played by the bald and bulky wrestler, Tor Johnson. Myron Healy is the detective who poses as an escaped murderer in order to gain access to the old manor. Carradine offers him sanctuary in exchange for volunteering for glandular treatment in the furtherance of his quest. Healy witnesses Carradine conducting an experiment on Sally Todd, who immediately ages a hundred years. This prompts him to free the lovely Allison Hayes in time to witness Carradine killed by one of his more horrid victims in a rare moment of lucidity. The British release print seemed horrible enough, but what happened in the five minutes that the censor cut out?

From Hell It Came

starring
TOD ANDREWS · TINA CARVER
with LINDA WATKINS · JOHN McNAMARA

AN
ALLIED ARTISTS
PICTURE

SCREENPLAY BY
Richard Bernstein · MILNER BROS.
PRODUCTION

DIRECTED BY
Dan Milner

PRODUCED BY
Jack Milner

From Hell It Came

1957 Milner Brothers
Distributor Allied Artists
Producer Jack Milner
Director Dan Milner
Story Richard Bernstein, Jack Milner
Screenplay Richard Bernstein
Camera Brydon Baker
Editor Jack Milner
Art Director Rudi Feld
Music Darrell Calker
70 minutes

Tod Andrews *Dr William Arnold*
Tina Carver *Dr Terry Mason*
Linda Watkins *Mrs Kilgore*
John McNamara *Dr Howard Clark*
Gregg Palmer *Kimo*
Robert Swan *Tano*
Baynes Barron *Chief Maranka*

One of the odder entries in the B-horror stakes was this tale of treachery, revenge and walking wood, set on the sun-drenched tropical paradise of the Island of Kalai. A suspicious conspiracy between Chief Maranka, Witch Doctor Tano and his faithless wife causes the innocent Kimo to be condemned to unpleasant death. Before he expires, Kimo vows he will return from the grave to wreak vengeance. This he does in the form of an animated yet ancient tree stump, a killer with branches everywhere. The perambulating trunk is befriended by Dr Terry Mason, a lady biologist, and her small party of scientists, who seek the root of his trouble. The tree breaks free from their care and sets about its mission of revenge, carrying off its avowed victims and dumping them in a swamp. The decent scientists will have none of this and proceed to hunt down the tree, pursuing it into the bog leaving only a willow to weep.

in her eyes.... DESIRE!
in her veins....
the blood of a MONSTER!

BLOOD OF DRACULA

WILL GIVE YOU NIGHTMARES FOREVER

Starring Sandra HARRISON · Louise LEWIS · GAIL GANLEY · JERRY BLAINE

Produced by HERMAN COHEN · Directed by HERBERT L. STROCK · Screenplay by RALPH THORNTON

A JAMES H. NICHOLSON-SAMUEL Z. ARKOFF PRODUCTION · AN AMERICAN INTERNATIONAL PICTURE

Blood of Dracula

UK title Blood is my Heritage
1957 American International
Executive Producers
    James H. Nicholson, Samuel Z. Arkoff
Producer Herman Cohen
Director Herbert L. Strock
Screenplay Ralph Thornton
Camera Monroe Askins
Art Director Leslie Thomas
Editor Robert Moore
Music Paul Dunlap
Assistant Director Austen Jewell
69 minutes

Sandra Harrison *Nancy Perkins*
Louise Lewis *Miss Branding*
Gail Ganley *Myra*
Jerry Blaine *Tab*
Heather Ames *Nola*
Malcolm Atterbury *Lt Dunlap*
Mary Adams *Mrs Thorndyke*
Thomas Browne Henry *Mr Perkins*
Don Devlin *Eddie*
Richard Devon

'Will Give You Nightmares Forever!' claimed the lobby cards. A little exaggerated, I feel; I saw the film in 1957 and haven't had a nightmare yet. However, here we have perhaps the beginnings of the teenage horror cycle, produced by Herman Cohen who later consolidated his success with teenage werewolves, Frankensteins, et al. Teenage teenager, Sandra Harrison, is sent to a girls' school against her wishes, and promptly takes a dislike to her attractive young classmates, as do they her. Chemistry mistress Louise Lewis promises to give Sandra control over her emotions if she will but submit to an odd experiment involving the use of an amulet which, she says, has occult powers. Sandra agrees, and under Miss Lewis's lure she grows a pair of startling eyebrows and a set of unattractively deformed teeth. The girl has transformed into a vampire! She kills several of her fellow boarders in her lust for living blood, each time returning to normal with no memory of what she has done. Sandra gets the urge to kill her own boyfriend, and pleads with Miss Lewis for release. The evil teacher refuses, so Sandra changes into the vampire and kills her before dying herself during the struggle for the strange amulet.

Teenage Zombies

1957 GBM Productions
Distributor Governor Films
Producer Jerry Warren
Director Jerry Warren
Screenplay Jacques Lecotier
Camera Allen Chandler
Music Erich Bromberg
Makeup Jean Morrison
74 minutes

Don Sullivan *Regg*
Katherine Victor *Dr. Myra*
Steve Conte *Wharf*
Paul Pepper *Skip*
Bri Murphy *Pam*
Mitzie Albertson *Julie*
Jay Hawk *Morrie*
Nan Green *Dot*
J.L.D. Morrison *Brandt*
Mike Concannen *Sheriff*
Chuck Niles *Ivan*
Don Neeley *Major Coleman*

Four teenagers (according to the *Monthly Film Bulletin*) or six teenagers (according to *Willis's Horror and Science Fiction Films*) take a water-skiing holiday and land on a mysterious island where they are promptly taken prisoner by Ivan the Ape Man. Katherine Victor plays the attractive exotic Doctor Myra who locks the young explorers away in cages while she gets on with the job of converting humans into zombies. To do this she is experimenting with a nerve gas, financed by 'Another Power' which intends to use the gas as a military weapon and thus conquer the world. Meanwhile the teenagers' teenage chums, missing their buddies, tell the cops they are missing, which prompts the local Sheriff into investigating. Unfortunately the Sheriff is in fact also in the foreign power's employ. It is he who is supplying the doctor with subjects for her experiments. The Sheriff gets shot, the teenagers escape, and Ivan the Ape Man destroys the evil laboratory. The End.

AN ALLIED ARTISTS PICTURE

THE BRIDE AND THE BEAST

starring
LANCE FULLER · CHARLOTTE AUSTIN

with Johnny Roth · William Justine
Jeanne Gerson

PRODUCED AND DIRECTED BY   SCREENPLAY BY
ADRIAN WEISS · EDWARD D. WOOD, JR.

Production Supervised by LOUIS WEISS

An ADRIAN WEISS Production

The Bride and The Beast

1957 Weiss Productions
Distributor Allied Artists
Executive Producer Louis Weiss
Producer Adrian Weiss
Director Adrian Weiss
Story Adrian Weiss
Screenplay Edward D. Wood Jr
Camera Roland Price
Editor George Merrick
Art Director Edward Shiells
Music Les Baxter
78 (75) minutes

Lance Fuller Dan
Charlotte Austin Laura
Johnny Roth Taro
William Justine Dr Reiner
Jeanne Gerson Marka
Steve Calvert The Beast

Dan and Laura, newlywed big-game hunters, are honeymooning in the depths of the jungle when, much to his surprise, Dan discovers his pet gorilla making curious advances to his bride on their wedding night. Seeing no immediate alternative, Dan promptly shoots the animal, an action which rather disturbs his wife. Dan takes her to see Dr Reiner, a local hypnotist, under whose influence Laura learns that she is actually the reincarnation of a gorilla. Having made her confront her strange past, the doctor declares her cured, and hubby bears her away on safari. He is immediately wounded by a tiger, while a giant gorilla, getting a whiff of Laura, kidnaps her and bears her away to his tribal cave for inspection by his buddies. Dan takes off after her, rifle ready for the rescue, but is shocked when Laura and her gorilla attack back. Disillusioned by the fickleness of women, Dan returns home, sadder, wiser, lonelier. Made with the help of Steve Calvert and his monkey suit, plus several reels of jungle footage from *Man-Eater of Kumaon*, this film is perhaps the least seen of Edward D. Wood Junior's *oeuvre*, and perhaps that is just as well.

The Vampire's Coffin

Original title El Ataud del Vampiro
1957 Cinematografica Absa
Distributor Young America Productions
Producer Abel Salazar
US Producer K. Gordon Murray
Director Fernando Mendez
US Director Paul Nagle
Story Raul Zenteno
Screenplay Raul Zenteno, Ramon Obon,
                         Enrique Rodriguez
Camera Victor Herrera
US Camera Kurt Dayton
Art Director Gunther Gerszo
US Art Director William Hayden
Music Gustavo Carrion
86 minutes Hypnoscope

Abel Salazar Dr Enrique
German Robles Count Karol de Lavud
Ariadna Welter Marta
Alicia Montoya Maria Teresa
Yerye Beirute
Guillermo Orea
Carlos Anicra
Antonio Raxell

Mexican movie made in the mould of the bygone Universal City style: black and white vampires stalking among the swirling mists of the graveyards, then changing into outsize bats to suck the life-giving blood from the necks of their victims. Period stuff for the Fifties, but just what the Mexican audiences ordered, especially now that Hollywood was knee-deep in atomic monsters. Yankee showman K. Gordon Murray thought the Stateside small-towners would like it too, and doctored up the picture with the aid of director Paul Nagle. Then he branded the result 'Recommended by the Young America Horror Club', a gimmick he himself invented. He pretended the film was in Hypnoscope ("Thru the Power of Hypnosis It Will Heighten the Horror!') and cleaned up a small fortune. Unfortunately it did not do much good for the movie, which was a highly expert and well-made horror picture bringing back the supposedly deceased-by-stake vampire, Count Karol de Lavud, 'hero' of the 1957 El Vampiro, and setting him up in a deserted wax museum. The film was double-billed with another Mexican movie, the science-fiction mixup entitled The Robot Versus the Aztec Mummy.

THE GRAVE CAN'T HOLD IT

...nothing human can stop it!

...it rose from the crypt to slake its monstrous thirst for beauty...and the power to rule the earth!

THE THING THAT COULDN'T DIE

Starring

WILLIAM REYNOLDS · ANDRA MARTIN · CAROLYN KEARNEY · JEFFREY STONE

WRITTEN BY DAVID DUNCAN · PRODUCED AND DIRECTED BY WILL COWAN · A UNIVERSAL-INTERNATIONAL PICTURE

The Thing That Couldn't Die

1958 Universal International
Producer Will Cowan
Director Will Cowan
Screenplay David Duncan
Camera Russell Metty
Special Effects Clifford Stine
Art Director Alexander Golitzen
Editor Edward Curtiss
Music Joseph Gershenson
69 minutes

William Reynolds *Gordon Hawthorne*
Andra Martin *Linda Madison*
Carolyn Kearney *Jessica Burns*
Jeffrey Stone *Hank Huston*
Charles Horvath *Mike*
James Anderson *Boyd Abercrombie*
Robin Hughes
Forrest Lewis

'It rose from the crypt to slake its montrous thirst for beauty . . . and the power to rule the earth!' Alternative slogan: if you want to get ahead, get a head. The Thing that couldn't die turns out to be the decapitated head of a 400-year-old sailor, located in mistake for water by Andra Martin, diviner. Living in a lonely old ranch in the California wastelands, Miss Martin's odd powers lead her to unearth a buried chest which, when opened, contains a severed head. The legend tells of an Elizabethan sailor, a member of Magellan's expedition back in 1579, who practised devil worship. For this Satanism he was beheaded by Sir Francis Drake, and his separate bits buried apart. Miss Martin must now locate the torso, and with the aid of her bent twig she does just that. When the eye-rolling, mutter-mouthed head is united again with its body, instead of walking the world once again it crumbles to dust, thanks to the timely use of an ancient talisman. This horror programmer was produced and directed by Will Cowan, who had made a string of jolly B-musicals for Universal back in the wartime Forties, and should gave stayed there.

Frankenstein 1970

1958 Allied Artists
Producer Aubrey Schenck
Director Howard W. Koch
Story Aubrey Schenck, Charles Moss
Screenplay Richard Landau,
George Worthing Yates
Camera Carl Guthrie
Editor Jack Bushelman
Art Director Jack Collis
Music Paul Dunlap
Makeup Gordon Bau
83 minutes CinemaScope

Boris Karloff *Baron von Frankenstein*
Tom Duggan *Mike Shaw*
Lana Lund *Carolyn Hayes*
Donald Barry *Douglas Row*
Charlotte Austin *Judy Stevens*
James Anderson *Boyd Abercrombie*
Irwin Berke *Inspector Raab*
Rudolph Anders *Wilhelm Gottfried*
John Dennis *Morgan Haley*
Norbert Schiller *Shuter*
Mike Lane *Hans*

'The One, the Only King of the Monsters as the New Demon of the Atomic Age!' The lobby card wanted you to think they meant Boris Karloff as the Frankenstein Monster, of course. But he wasn't. For the first time he played a true Frankenstein, Baron Victor von, latest in a long line of monster makers, complete with facial scars sustained during the war, it seems, at the hands of Nazi torturers. The Monster, seen from the back only on the lobby cards, certainly had the build of Boris in the 1931 classic, but was played by one Mike Lane. Lurching into the Fifties (the title, setting the story twelve years ahead was a mere gimmick, never being referred to in the film itself), the famous Monster is revived by the old Baron after selling the television rights to an American crew. He spends the cash on a portable atomic reactor which he has delivered to the back door of his castle so the lodgers don't see. Installing it in his cellar laboratory, the Baron is forced the kill off a visitor or two to obtain some fresh body parts, but finally the creature is completed and, held together by bandages, goes on a sightless rampage in the best family tradition. In that same tradition, both he and old Boris perish, of course.

ALL NEW and MORE HORRIFIC THAN BEFORE!

RETURN of the FLY

CINEMASCOPE

STARRING

VINCENT PRICE

AND

BRETT HALSEY · JOHN SUTTON
DAVID FRANKHAM · DAN SEYMOUR

PRODUCED BY
BERNARD GLASSER · EDWARD L. BERNDS

DIRECTED FROM HIS SCREENPLAY BY

BASED UPON GEORGE LANGELAAN'S
SHORT STORY "THE FLY"

PRODUCED BY ASSOCIATED PRODUCERS, INC.

RELEASED BY 20th CENTURY-FOX FILM CORPORATION

Return of the Fly

1959 Associated Producers
Distributor Twentieth Century Fox
Producer Bernard Glasser
Director Edward Bernds
Story based on *The Fly* by
    George Langelaan
Screenplay Edward Bernds
Camera Brydon Baker
Art Director Lyle Wheeler
Editor Richard Meyer
Music Paul Sawtell, Bert Shefter
80 minutes CinemaScope

Vincent Price *Francois Delambre*
Brett Halsey *Phillippe Delambre*
John Sutton *Inspector Beauchamp*
David Frankham *Alan Hinds*
Dan Seymour *Max Berthold*
Danielle De Metz *Cecile Bonnard*

'All New and More Horrific than Before!' cried the lobby card, with a wobbly accent on the Horrific. This was the sequel to Fox's major box-office success of 1958, *The Fly*, which took its story from the famous *Playboy* short novella written by George Langelaan. Like most sequels, indeed like almost all sequels, this one was cut-price, cut-rate, and made another bomb! Set in a curious Montreal, it told of young handsome Brett Halsey who, as the scientist's child of the previous year, has now grown rather swiftly into handsome manhood. He is determined to continue dead dad's experiments and to this end rebuilds the famous matter transmitter despite the dread warnings of his father's old friend, Vincent Price. His assistant, however, is secretly working for another faction and causes things to go wrong. With a spot of swift trickery he causes Halsey to be changed into the now familiar monster fly, forgetting, apparently, how fiendish this creature can be. It kills the spy, and the chap who hired him, before good old Vincent gets the machinery going again to convert him back into his original components. For once, a happy ending. But wait – in six years time there will follow *The Curse of the Fly!*

STARRING **BEVERLY GARLAND** · **BRUCE BENNETT** · **LON CHANEY** · **GEORGE MACREADY**
AND **FRIEDA INESCORT** · RICHARD CRANE · DOUGLAS KENNEDY

PRODUCED BY JACK LEEWOOD · ROY DEL RUTH · DIRECTED BY ORVILLE H. HAMPTON SCREENPLAY BY

CinemaScope

THE **ALLIGATOR PEOPLE**

PRODUCED BY ASSOCIATED PRODUCERS, Inc. 20th CENTURY-FOX

The Alligator People

1959 Associated Producers
Distributor Twentieth Century Fox
Producer Jack Leewood
Director Roy Del Ruth
Story Charles O'Neal
Screenplay Orville Hampton
Camera Karl Struss
Special Effects Fred Etcheverry
Editor Harry Gerstad
Art Director Lyle Wheeler
Music Irving Gertz
74 minutes

Beverly Garland *Joyce Webster*
Bruce Bennett *Dr Eric Lorimer*
Lon Chaney *Mannon*
George Macready *Dr Mark Sinclair*
Frieda Inescort *Mrs Hawthorne*
Richard Crane *Paul Webster*
Douglas Kennedy *Dr Wayne McGregor*

Way down in the Louisiana swamps, suave-spoken George Macready has an idea. If reptiles can regrow those bits of their bodies which have been amputated, why not humans? Especially those who have been maimed by war. He tries out his extract of alligator on Richard Crane, mutilated aviator, and it works. Delighted, the mended man promptly weds his attractive nurse, Beverly Garland. Unfortunately reversion begins to occur, and on his wedding night Crane becomes part-croc, his skin thickening and cracking, his teeth growing alarmingly pointed. Hoping a dose of gamma rays might cure his condition, Crane flees into the swamps, but by the time Miss Garland finds him he is not just part-croc, he is half-croc. He perishes in a quagmire and Miss Garland loses her reason, and who shall blame her? Especially when, to add to her unusual troubles, hook-handed Lon Chaney is lurking about waiting to rape her. The old 'wolf-man' was present in the cast as a useful box-office name; those who expected him to change into an alligator were doomed to disappointment. The film was something of a swamp-song for two major movie talents, Roy Del Ruth, who had risen from Mack Sennett gaggery to direct some great stuff for Warner Brothers, and Karl Struss, the old German who had photographed the 1932 version of *Dr Jekyll and Mr Hyde*.

COLUMBIA PICTURES presents

The Tingler

starring **VINCENT PRICE**

with JUDITH EVELYN

A WILLIAM CASTLE PRODUCTION

filmed in **PERCEPTO!**

The Tingler

1959 Castle Pictures
Distributor Columbia Pictures
Producer William Castle
Director William Castle
Associate Producer Dona Holloway
Screenplay Robb White
Camera Wilfrid Cline
Art Director Phil Bennett
Editor Chester Schaeffer
Music Von Dexter
82 minutes Percepto

Vincent Price *Dr William Chapin*
Judith Evelyn *Mrs Higgins*
Darryl Hickman *David Morris*
Patricia Cutts *Isabel Chapin*
Pamela Lincoln *Lucy Stevens*
Philip Collidge *Ollie Higgins*
William Castle *Himself*

The third in producer/director William Castle's series of shockers-with-a-gimmick. Following the 3-D craze in which audiences were surrounded by cinematic action, Castle reversed the procedure by putting the action among the audience. He wired certain seats in every cinema with war surplus vibrators, having them set off at pre-ordained signals and thus scaring the pants off his patrons. He called this process Percepto, and as if that was not enough, had a bath of blood tinted red in his otherwise monochrome movie. American audiences experienced a further exciting plus when attendants ran down the theatre aisle with a stretcher to carry out a screaming usherette! The theme of the movie is that Price, as a pathologist, isolates the creature that causes fright in humans, a scaly lobsterish thing that wraps itself around the spine. He plucks a fine specimen from the corpse of a widow who owns a silent cinema, but it escapes and crawls over the audience's feet during a performance of *Tol'able David*. His wife, played by the beauteous but ultimately tragic British star, Patricia Cutts, tries to kill him with the Tingler while he dozes, but a well-timed scream from sister-in-law Lucy saves him. An original but utterly silly film, it loses all its Percepto points when played on television.

THE DEAD ONE

Exotic VooDoo Rituals

STARRING LINDA ORMOND · JOHN MACKAY WITH CLYDE KELLEY · DARLENE MYRICK · MONICA DAVIS
BARRY MAHON EXECUTIVE PRODUCER BRANDON CHASE

PRODUCED AND DIRECTED BY

A PRESENTATION OF MARDI GRAS PRODUCTIONS, INC. ULTRASCOPE EASTMAN COLOR

The Dead One

1960 Mardi Gras Productions
Executive Producer Brandon Chase
Producer Barry Mahon
Director Barry Mahon
Screenplay Barry Mahon
Camera Mark Dennes
Editor Alan Smiler
Art Director Stanley Raines
71 minutes Eastmancolour Ultrascope

Linda Ormond *Linda Mackay*
John Mackay *John Mackay*
Clyde Kelley *Jonas*
Darlene Myrick *Bella Bella*
Monica Davis *Monica*

John and Linda, newlyweds, spend a hot time in the old town of New Orleans, taking in a spot of strip-tease and similar stuff before driving off to the family plantation for their honeymoon. On the way they give a lift to Bella Bella the Belly Dancer (believe it or not), and invite her to stay the night, an unusual gesture for a honeymoon couple. John's cousin Monica receives them rather coldly, as his marriage has caused her to lose her rights in the property. To get her own back she uses a little voodoo to revive the dead body of her brother Jonas. A deathly white zombie in natty gents evening dress, Jonas murders Bella Bella in mistake for John, which just shows what the grave will do for a man's mind. John puts in a call for the cops, and they arrive in time to shoot Monica as she tries to protect her zombie brother. Jonas disintegrates as he walks into the light of the sun, and John puts the plantation up for sale.

MEL ELSA ANNETTE
FERRER MARTINELLI VADIM

in Roger Vadim's

BLOOD and ROSES

TECHNICOLOR®
TECHNIRAMA®

Screenplay by ROGER VADIM and ROGER VAILLAND · Produced by RAYMOND EGER · A Paramount Release

Blood and Roses

Original title Et Mourir de Plaisir
1960 Films EGE/Documento Film
Distributor Paramount Pictures
Producer Raymond Eger
Director Roger Vadim
Story from Carmilla by Sheridan le Fanu
Screenplay Roger Vadim,
Roger Vailland,
Claude Brule,
Claude Martin
Dialogue Roger Vailland, Peter Viertel
Camera Claude Renoir
Editor Victoria Mercanton
Art Director Jean André
Music Jean Prodomides
87 minutes Technicolor Technirama

Mel Ferrer Leopoldo De Karnstein
Elsa Martinelli Georgia Monteverdi
Annette Vadim Carmilla
Marc Allgeret Judge Monteverdi
Jacques-Rene Chauffard Dr Verari
Alberto Bonucci Carlo Ruggieri
Serge Marquand Giuseppi
Renato Speziali Guido Naldi
Gabriella Farinon Lisa
Camilla Stroyberg Martha
Nathalie Le Foret Marie
Edythe Arlene Catalano Cook
Dianni Di Benedetto Marshal

The first of many variations by modern film-makers founded on Sheridan Le Fanu's classic short story, Carmilla, favoured no doubt for its erotic blending of vampirism and lesbianism. The female breast is far more photogenic for sinking one's fangs into than the neck; more delicious too. Roger Vadim, popular for his 'art house' erotics in the Sixties, wrote and directed this elegant and expensive affair, shorn of two naughty minutes by the British censor, who still awarded the film an 'X' certificate. Set in contemporary Rome, the country seat of the Karnsteins is cursed by the ghost of Millarca, who kills off the loved ladies of all male descendants. During the latest Karnstein's engagement party, a firework sets off a buried cache of German munitions which, in due turn, release Millarca's spirit once again, this time through the physical body of Karnstein's cousin Carmilla. The effect on the young girl is fiendish: her hands are cold, the flowers she touches wither, her horse whinnies away from her, and she can no longer stand the sunshine. After an attack on Georgia's left breast, Carmilla gets blown up by some more German munitions and dies with a fence post driven accidentally through her heart. All seems well for Karnstein's honeymoon; he fails to notice that the rose his bride is holding is losing its petals, one by one.

...BY THE SHE-GHOST OF HAUNTED ISLAND!

TORMENTED

Starring **RICHARD CARLSON**

JULI REDING · SUSAN GORDON
LUGENE SANDERS · JOE TURKEL

Produced by BERT I. GORDON
Directed by BERT I. GORDON
and JOE STEINBERG
Screenplay by GEORGE WORTHING YATES
An ALLIED ARTISTS Picture

Tormented

1960 Cheviot Productions
Distributor Allied Artists
Producer Bert I. Gordon, Joe Steinberg
Director Bert I. Gordon
Story Bert I. Gordon
Screenplay George Worthing Yates
Camera Ernest Laszlo
Special Effects Bert I. Gordon,
    Flora Gordon
Art Director Gabriel Scognamillo
Music Albert Glasser
Editor John Bushelman
Assistant Director Bill Forsyth
75 (62) minutes

Richard Carlson *Tom Stewart*
Juli Reding *Vi*
Susan Gordon *Sandy*
Lugene Sanders *Meg*
Joe Turkel *Nick*
Lillian Adams *Estate Agent*
Gene Roth *Lunch Stand Owner*
Vera Marsh *Mother*
Harry Fleer *Father*
Merritt Stone *Clergyman*

Richard Carlson, no stranger to lower case sci-fi and horror pictures, appears here as a jazz pianist (special jazz score by Calvin Jackson) who rejects his clinging mistress, Meg, for the even shorter named but definitely wealthier Vi. Meg promptly falls off a lighthouse, but returns to life, smothered in seaweed, to haunt the lovers in their island hideaway. She causes all manner of spiritual disturbances, soaking Vi's wedding dress with seaweed, appearing rather startlingly between them in personal photographs of the pair, trailing her perfume about the place, and leaving bare footsteps in the sand. She is at the wedding ceremony, too, bursting open the door with invisible strength and causing the minister's prayer book to open at the Burial Service. Carlson has had enough. He murders a blackmailing boatman and is about to chuck his wife's precious ten-year-old sister (played by the director's precocious ten-year-old daughter) off the lighthouse when Meg materialises once more. He falls to his death and when his body is recovered from the sea it is in the loving embrace of Meg's corpse. Despite chopping thirteen minutes of horror out of this film, the British censor still gave it an 'X' Certificate.

BLACK SUNDAY

starring BARBARA STEELE · JOHN RICHARDSON · IVO GARRANI · ANDREA CHECCHI Directed by MARIO BAVA · AN AMERICAN-INTERNATIONAL PICTURE

A GALATEA-JOLLY FILM PRODUCTION

PLEASE NOTE

The producers of BLACK SUNDAY recommend that it be seen only by those over 12 years of age!

STARE INTO THESE EYES

discover deep within them the unspeakable terrifying secret of "BLACK SUNDAY"

Black Sunday

Original title La Maschera Del Demonio
UK title Revenge of the Vampire
1960 Galatea/Jolly Films
Distributor American International
Producer Massimo De Rita
Director Mario Bava
Story based on The Vij by Nikolai Gogol
Screenplay Ennio de Concini,
  Mario Bava,
  Marcello Coscia,
  Mario Serandrei
Adaptation Marcello Coscia
Camera Ubaldo Terzano, Mario Bava
Art Director Giorgio Giovannini
Editor Mario Serandrei
Music Roberto Nicolosi
US Music Les Baxter
88 minutes

Barbara Steele Katia/Princess Asa
John Richardson Andrej
Ivo Garrani Prince Vajda
Andrea Checchi Dr Kruvajan
Arturo Dominici Javutich
Clara Bindi Innkeeper
Enrico Olivieri Constantine
Mario Passante Nikita
Germana Dominici Peasant
Tino Bianchi Ivan
Antonio Pierfederici
Renato Terra

Barbara Steele, J. Arthur Rank's lost bit-player, turned up in Italy all raven tresses and staring eyes to claim a permanent place in the horror film repertory company and the world-wide worship of young lads in their pimples. Her opening scene is one of the great shocks of the genre when, as a seventeenth-century witch about to be burned at the stake, her head is thrust into an iron mask and the internal spikes are hammered home. Two hundred years later a doctor chances to cut his hand while examining her tomb, and a drop of his blood brings her back to life. With her revived accomplice Javutich, she proceeds to take over the physical body of her descendant and double, Princess Katia (also Miss Steele). This distresses her brother, who is about the destroy the lifeless body of Katia when he notices she is still wearing her crucifix. Realising she cannot be the vampire, he locates the real witch, stakes her heartily, and Katia is restored to life. A great favourite with cineastes, the film was finally shown in the UK after being held up by the censor for eight years.

AMERICAN INTERNATIONAL PRESENTS

EDGAR ALLAN POE'S

THE PIT AND THE PENDULUM

IN PANAVISION AND COLOR

MUSIC BY LES BAXTER

PRODUCED AND DIRECTED BY ROGER CORMAN

SCREENPLAY BY RICHARD MATHESON

STARRING VINCENT PRICE · JOHN KERR · BARBARA STEELE · LUANA ANDERS

The Pit and the Pendulum

1961 Alta Vista Productions
Distributor American International
Executive Producers James H. Nicholson,
Samuel Z. Arkoff
Producer Roger Corman
Director Roger Corman
Story from the short story by
Edgar Allan Poe
Screenplay Richard Matheson
Camera Floyd Crosby
Special Effects Larry Butler,
Don Glouer, Pat Dinga
Art Director Daniel Haller
Editor Anthony Carras
Music Les Baxter
Makeup Ted Cooley
85 minutes Pathecolor Panavision

Vincent Price *Nicholas Medina*
John Kerr *Francis Barnard*
Barbara Steele *Elizabeth*
Luana Anders *Catherine*
Anthony Carbone *Dr Charles Leon*
Patrick Westwood *Maximillian*
Lynne Bernay *Maria*
Larry Turner *Nicholas (child)*
Mary Menzies *Isabella*
Charles Victor *Bartolome*

'This was my father's life,' explains Vincent Price, a hint of madness in his rolling eye as he takes his young visitor from England, John Kerr, to see his subterranean torture chamber. Following the great success of his *Fall of the House of Usher*, Roger Corman returns to Edgar Allan Poe-land, this time set in sixteenth-century Spain, for another outing with his new team of writer, photographer, composer, and co. Plus, of course, star. Poe brought a new lease of life to the long career of Vincent Price, gourmet, art collector, and actor, making him the best box-office star in the horror genre since Boris Karloff. Despite their length (this one was shortened by five minutes, thanks to the British censor), their sumptuousness, and their slightly ponderous pace, Corman's efforts in the 'A' class of movie remained solidly 'B' class, with minimal casts (a star to go mad, two juveniles to fall in love, a butler and a family doctor), simple sets (corridors, chambers, and corridors) and dream sequences, punctuated by exteriors of castles on cliffs used as chapter breaks. Nice to see cult queen Barbara Steele on the third leg of her career: Pinewood, Italy and now Hollywood.

"WITHIN THE COFFIN
I LIE... ALIVE!"

AMERICAN–INTERNATIONAL PRESENTS

IN COLOR AND PANAVISION®

RAY MILLAND

EDGAR ALLAN POE's

THE PREMATURE BURIAL

STARRING IN HAZEL COURT · RICHARD NEY · HEATHER ANGEL

CO-STARRING CHARLES BEAUMONT & RAY RUSSELL

Produced and Directed by ROGER CORMAN

The Premature Burial

1961 Filmgroup/Santa Clara
Distributor American International
Executive Producers Gene Corman
Producer Roger Corman
Director Roger Corman
Story from the short story by
    Edgar Allan Poe
Screenplay Charles Beaumont
    Ray Russell
Camera Floyd Crosby
Art Director Daniel Haller
Editor Ronald Sinclair
Music Ronald Stein
81 minutes Pathecolor Panavision

Ray Milland *Guy Carrell*
Hazel Court *Emily Gault*
Richard Ney *Miles Archer*
Heather Angel *Kate Carrell*
Alan Napier *Dr Gideon Gault*
John Dierkes *Sweeney*
Richard Miller *Mole*
Brendon Dillon *Minister*

The third of Roger Corman's tales from Poe suffers from being cut-price. Instead of Vincent of that ilk, an actor adept at expressing a haunted persona, we have stolid old Ray Milland, ever too well fed to suffer from horrors that were not direct from the bottle. An Oscar for portraying a drunk is no recommendation for demonstrating fears of burial alive. Convinced that his late father was entombed whilst suffering a mere cataleptic fit, Milland feels certain that he too will end his days trying to claw his way out of a closed coffin. To this end he builds his own tomb, equipped with cunning escape devices. Young Dr Archer persuades him to open his father's tomb in an attempt to pacify his fears, but the scrabbling thing that falls out sends Milland into an immediate trance. Pronounced dead, he is duly buried but returns from the grave a mad murderer. Had the film been blessed with Price, a more than minor classic might have been the result. However, we must be thankful for the chance to see two bonny British lasses, the fading Heather Angel from the Thirties and the burgeoning Hazel Court from the Forties.

THE WITCH'S CURSE

IN COLOR

starring KIRK MORRIS / HELENE CHANEL A MEDALLION PICTURES RELEASE

FOR 100 YEARS THE WITCH'S CURSE HUNG LIKE A SHROUD OVER THE VILLAGE...

The Witch's Curse

Original title Maciste All' Inferno
1962 Panda Films
Distributor Medallion Pictures
Producers Luigi Carpentieri,
    Ermanno Donati
Director Riccardo Freda
Screenplay Oreste Biancoli,
    Piero Pierotti,
    Ennio de Concini,
    Ermanno Donati
Story Eddy Given, Guido Brignore
Camera Riccardo Pallotini
Special Effects Serge Urbisaglia
Art Director Andrew Crizanti
Editor Ornella Micheli
Music Carlo Franci
90 (78) minutes Colorscope

Kirk Morris *Maciste*
Helene Chanel *Matha Gunt*
·Vira Silenti *Matha (child)*
Andrea Bosic *Parris*
Angelo Zanolli *Charley Law*
John Karlson *Burgomaster*
John Francis Lane *Coachman*
Neil Robinson *Villager*
Charles Fawcett *Doctor*

'For 100 years the Witch's Curse hung like a shroud over the village' intoned the lobby cards. Unfortunately, the village was supposed to be in Scotland, which was a cue for much merriment among the audience. For this was a village of pine trees and terraced houses with whitewashed walls, a location easier to find in sunny Italy where, of course, this picture was produced. It was one of a dozen or more strong-man sagas featuring the legendary hero Maciste, here played by musclebound Kirk Morris, one of the innumerable plexus-flexers raised to temporary stardom by the Italian film industry. This time Maciste voyages into the Scottish underworld to seek out a witch and thus remove her curse from an attractive descendant. Along the way Maciste throws a boulder or two between clips from his earlier adventures. Even with severe shortening by the English language distributors (from 90 minutes to 78), the film still seemed far too long.

BLACK ZOO

MICHAEL **GOUGH** · JEANNE **COOPER** · ROD **LAUREN** · VIRGINIA **GREY**

A HERMAN COHEN PRODUCTION STARRING

screenplay by ABEN KANDEL and HERMAN COHEN · directed by ROBERT GORDON · produced by HERMAN COHEN

AN ALLIED ARTISTS PICTURE

IN BLOOD-CURDLING **COLOR** AND **PANAVISION**

FANG AND CLAW KILLERS STALK THE CITY STREETS!

Black Zoo

1963 Allied Artists
Producer Herman Cohen
Director Robert Gordon
Screenplay Herman Cohen,
    Aben Kandel
Camera Floyd Crosby
Special Effects Pat Dinga
Art Director William Glasgow
Editor Michael Luciano
Music Paul Dunlap
88 minutes Eastmancolor Panavision

Michael Gough *Michael Conrad*
Jeanne Cooper *Edna Conrad*
Rod Lauren *Carl*
Virginia Grey *Jenny*
Jerome Cowan *Jeffrey Stengel*
Elisha Cook Jr *Joe*
Warene Ott *Mary Hogan*
Marianna Hill *Audrey*
Oren Curtis *Radu*
Eilene Janssen *Bride*
Eric Stone *Groom*
Dani Lynn *Student*
Susan Slavin *Student*
Edward Platt *Detective Rivers*
Douglas Henderson *Lt Duggan*
Jerry Douglas *Technician*
Claudia Brack *Mother*
Daniel Kurlick *Carl (child)*
Byron Morrow *Coroner*
Michael St Angel *Officer Donovan*

Michael Gough, a British actor never noted for underplaying, had the time of his life in this Hollywood horror, in a role that ensured that just once is his long career as a trusty support he had his name above the title. Hoping perhaps for another Vincent Price, quickie producer Cohen may have been disappointed, but he certainly got his moneysworth as Gough donned a tigerskin robe and draped his mad menagerie, a lion, a tiger, a panther and a cougar, around the easy chairs in his living-room and played them a lullaby on his mighty organ. Gough was cast as the owner of a private zoo in Los Angeles and member of the True Believers, a cult of animal worshippers who believe that their souls can be transferred with the souls of wild beasts. He uses his weird power over animals to have them kill a speculator, a sadistic keeper, a chimp trainer and so on, before his own mute son kills him.

The Terror

1963 Filmgroup
Distributor American International
Executive Producer Harvey Jacobson
Producer Roger Corman
Associate Producer Francis Coppola
Director Roger Corman, Monte Hellman
Screenplay Leo Gordon, Jack Hill
Camera John Nickolaus
Art Director Daniel Haller
Editor Stuart O'Brien
Music Ronald Stein
81 minutes Pathecolor Vistascope

Boris Karloff *Baron Von Leppe*
Jack Nicholson *André Duvalier*
Sandra Knight *Heléne*
Richard Miller *Stefan*
Dorothy Neumann *Witch*
Jonathan Haze *Gustaf*

'Inconceivable! Unbelievable!' cried the lobby cards, but when they referred to a Diabolical Plan of Torture coming from the Depths of an Evil Mind, did they mean Boris Karloff's or Roger Corman's? For this is the classic grade C B-movie that the busy young producer-director cooked up in an afternoon, shot in a couple of days which Karloff owed him (his last Corman movie having come in ahead of schedule), and padded out with another couple of days' location shooting by the ambitious Monte Hellman. And if the sets looked familiar, that is because they were, still standing around from *The Raven*. Young Jack Nicholson, son of American International boss James H., got his first break as a typical Corman hero, an officer in Napoleon's army lost along the Baltic coast. After a night in a witch's hovel, he is given shelter of a sort by Baron Karloff, still brooding over the death of his wife some twenty years earlier. The spectre of Sandra Knight can be seen flitting about the ruins, while Boris goes bonkers in the crypt doing his darnedest to drown himself. He turns out not to be the Baron after all, but the witch's son Erik, while Jack saves the solidly spectral Sandra only to have her turn into jelly in his embrace.

The Horror of Party Beach

1963 Inzom Productions
Distributor Twentieth Century Fox
Producers Del Tenney, Alan V. Iselin
Director Del Tenney
Screenplay Richard Hilliard
Camera Richard Hilliard
Editor Gary Youngman
Art Director Robert Verberkmoss
Music Bill Holmes
72 minutes

John Scott *Hank Green*
Alice Lyon *Elaine Gavin*
Allen Laurel *Dr Gavin*
Eulabelle Moore *Eulabelle*
Marilyn Clark *Tina*
Augustin Mayer *Mike*
Damon Kiebroyd *Lt Wells*
Monroe Wade *TV Announcer*
Sharon Murphy *Girl*
Carol Grubman *Girl*
The Del-Aires *Group*

From out of the depths they came, the repulsive radioactive monstrosities of this movie, and indeed the makers of this movie themselves. Lower than the lowest along Poverty Row, the low budget and lower talent team that called themselves Inzom Productions hired a few girls in swimming suits, paid a couple of pals to don monster outfits, and spent a weekend on a California beach with a camera. The resultant yarn about creatures created out of dumped radioactive waste who stomp out of the waves to murder a gang of girls, padded out with pop numbers by a phoney rock'n'roll group, was not worth the price of admission, even when double-billed with the same team's equally inept *Curse of the Living Corpse*. The glowing horrors are duly dealt with by Dr Gavin, who saves his daughter from slaughter by splattering them with unstable sodium. Possibly the world's worst double feature. Unless you know better!

Frankenstein Conquers the World

Original title Furankenshutain Tai Baragon
1965 Toho Productions
Distributor American International
Executive Producers Henry G. Saperstein,
    Reuben Bercovitch
Producer Tamoyuki Tanaka
Director Inoshiro Honda
Screenplay Kaoru Mabuchi
Camera Hajime Koizumi
Special Effects Eiji Tsuburaya
Art Director Takeo Kita
87 minutes Eastmancolor Tohoscope

Nick Adams *Dr James Bowen*
Tadao Takashima *Scientist*
Kumi Mizuno *Doctor*
Yoshio Tsuchiya
Takashi Shimura
Haruo Nakajima

One of the oddest slogans ever used on a lobby card graces this Japanese spectacular: 'He Rolled the Seven Wonders of the World into One!' Who did? When? How? And why? Could they mean Nick Adams, the youngish American star who made a few expatriate pictures before dying? Or director Honda or his special effects man Tsuburaya, who between them made Toho a household word for slam-bang sensationals. Never mind, meanwhile in the movie the living heart of Frankenstein's Monster is being shipped by submarine from Germany to Japan. It gets lost in the holocaust of the Hiroshima A-bomb. Twenty years later, the locals tell tales of a wild boy preying on their domesticated pets. Nick Adams, American medical scientist, catches the youth and is startled when the ugly thug starts growing at an alarming rate. In no time he is quite a giant, which enables him to break free, although he leaves behind a severed hand. Then out of a mighty earthquake, Baragon arrives on the scene, a giant prehistoric reptile freed from the bowels of the Earth by volcanic eruption. Young Frankenstein wades into the fight, slings the creature about by its tail, and as the entire Japanese army closes in with bombs and flame-throwers, kills the brute and is swallowed up by an earthquake. The monster boy's battle with an outsize octopus was excised, thus causing the American distributors to change the title from the original *Frankenstein Versus the Giant Devil Fish*.

WHAT WAS THE TERRIFYING SECRET OF THE VAMPIRE TREE?

You'll never forget.... THE CLUTCHING HORROR!

Island of the DOOMED

TECHNICOLOR® TECHNISCOPE®

starring CAMERON MITCHELL

Directed by MEL WELLES • An ALLIED ARTISTS Release

Island of the Doomed

Original title La Isla de la Muerte
UK title Bloodsuckers
1966 Orbita/Tefi
Distributors Allied Artists
Producer George Ferrer
(Ernst Von Theumer)
Director Mel Welles
(Ernst Von Theumer)
Story E.V. Theumer
Screenplay Stephen Schmidt,
Ira Meltcher
Camera Cecilio Paniagua
Editor Antonio Canovas
Art Director Francisco Canet
Music Anton Garcia Abril
88 (78) minutes Technicolor
Techniscope

Cameron Mitchell Baron von Weser
Elisa Montes Beth Christiansen
George Martin David Moss
Kai Fischer Julius Demerist
Rolf von Naukoff
Hermann Nehlsen
Matilde Sampredo
Mike Brendel
Riccardo Valle

'You'll Never Forget the Clutching Horror!' warned the lobby cards – but you'll certainly forget the movie! It told the tale of tourists who arrive on a small island offshore from Italy as house-guests in the mansion of Baron von Weser. The Baron (curious casting for Cameron Mitchell) owns a famous botanical garden from which are plucked strange fruits for the guests' dinner. These vegetarian party dishes repel the visitors: they taste strongly of meat. Small wonder, they are sliced from strange meat-eating plants which the Baron has created in his greenhouse. In the morning, two of his guests are found dead, their bodies drained of blood. Three further follow, until the killer is revealed as a tentacled tree that gorges on human blood with quite disgusting slurps. After an hour or so's slow suspense (the film is mercifully ten minutes shorter in its English edition), a whirling climax comes with hero and mad doctor hacking away at each other with axes, heroine screaming in the embrace of the vampire tree's tentacles, and great spouts of synthetic blood spraying hither and yon.

THE SHRIEKING of MUTILATED VICTIMS CAGED in a BLACK PIT of HORROR!

SHOCK by SHOCK YOU WILL FEEL THE CHILLING TERROR!

AMERICAN INTERNATIONAL'S

written & directed by Jack HILL & Stephanie ROTHMAN

produced by Jack HILL

BLOOD BATH

STARRING

William CAMPBELL * Marrisa MATHES * Linda SAUNDERS

Blood Bath

1966 American International
Executive Producer Roger Corman
Producer Jack Hill
Director Jack Hill, Stephanie Rothman
Screenplay Jack Hill,
        Stephanie Rothman
Camera Alfred Taylor
Editor Mort Tubor
Music Mark Lowery
80 (69) minutes

William Campbell Alberto Sordi
Marissa Mathes Daisy Allen
Lori Saunders Dorian/Melissa
Sandra Knight Donna Allen
Jonathan Haze

William Campbell is an artist of Italian extraction living among stock footage of Yugoslavia and the beach resort of Venice, California. He believes himself to be the reincarnation of a fifteenth-century vampire who was burned at the stake for his bloody misdeeds. He loves a young dancer and believes her to be a reincarnation, too. His vampire mania leads him to stalk attractive girls, making a start on his beloved's best friend. Luring her to his old bell-tower studio, he kills her, then dips her corpse into a vat of molten wax and paints her body. 'The Shrieking of Mutilated Victims Caged in a Black Pit of Horror!', as the lobby cards engagingly put it. In the end the waxed girls all come to life again and wreak suitable if inexplicable revenge. A confusing film, partly due to Corman's dismissal of Jack Hill during the manufacture, promoting scriptwriter Stephanie Rothman into the director's chair.